Finding Love after Loss

Finding Love after Loss

A Relationship Roadmap
for Widows

Marti Benedetti
and
Mary A. Dempsey

ROWMAN & LITTLEFIELD
Lanham • Boulder • New York • London

Published by Rowman & Littlefield
An imprint of The Rowman & Littlefield Publishing Group, Inc.
4501 Forbes Boulevard, Suite 200, Lanham, Maryland 20706
www.rowman.com

86-90 Paul Street, London EC2A 4NE, United Kingdom

British Library Cataloguing in Publication Information Available

Library of Congress Cataloging-in-Publication Data

Names: Benedetti, Marti, 1954- author. | Dempsey, Mary A., 1956- author.
Title: Finding love after loss : a relationship roadmap for widows / Marti
  Benedetti and Mary A. Dempsey.
Description: Lanham, Maryland : Rowman & Littlefield, an imprint of the
  Rowman & Littlefield Publishing Group, Inc., [2021] | Includes
  bibliographical references and index.
Identifiers: LCCN 2021017397 (print) | LCCN 2021017398 (ebook) | ISBN
  9781538152133 (cloth) | ISBN 9781538152140 (epub)
Subjects: LCSH: Widows—Social life and customs. | Dating (Social customs)
Classification: LCC HQ1058 .B46 2021 (print) | LCC HQ1058 (ebook) | DDC
  306.88/3—dc23
LC record available at https://lccn.loc.gov/2021017397
LC ebook record available at https://lccn.loc.gov/2021017398

To Tom, whom we adored.
To Dave, who helped us understand.
And to all the widows who shared their stories.

Contents

Acknowledgments

$\mathcal{A}$s journalists, we have always been drawn to people's stories. We are so, so grateful for the widows who graciously and generously offered us theirs. We were touched and informed by their frankness as they shared intimate details of their lives with their partners, their wrenching journeys through grief, and their determination to return to the bigger world. Their stories made us laugh and cry. Sometimes they made us gasp with surprise. And always they inspired and energized us with the thoughtful and creative ways these women were directing the next chapters of their lives.

We are thankful to the many other people who helped us see widowhood dating through *their* lens. These included widowers and the people in relationships with widows and widowers. They broadened our understanding of how new romance can be forged after searing loss, as well as the joys and tribulations that mark this journey.

We also appreciate the wise words of Tulane University professor Marilyn Mendoza. At the same time, our insider view of the operations of luxury matchmaking services would not have been possible without Lisa Hutcherson, vice president of client relations at Selective Search.

We are grateful to have had Suzanne Staszak-Silva as our editor at Rowman & Littlefield and to benefit from the careful work of her team, including Hannah Fisher, Crystal Clifton, and Deni Remsberg. To our agent, Maryann Karinch, for believing in our idea, thank you.

Other writer friends provided wise guidance on the direction of our book and read early chapters, offering spot-on advice. We also benefited from their editing suggestions. We are also especially grateful to Jane Barton-Griffith, Cheryl Bratz, Delinda Karle, Sarah Kellogg, Judy Putnam, Cynthia Wilcox, Melanie Deeds, Amy Hennes, Judy Ruskin, Barbara Porter, and Lisa Zagaroli.

And, finally, many thanks to all the friends, family members, and widows who encouraged us as we worked on this project.

Introduction

*T*his book was born out of a dinner conversation between two long-time friends. Marti was widowed and dipping her toes back into the dating scene, but trepidatious after so many years in a comfortable and joyful marriage. Mary, meanwhile, was a few years into a relationship with a widower who had met his wife in college and celebrated their thirty-second wedding anniversary before she died. Mary felt unskilled in navigating the ever-present sense of loss, sadness, and sometimes anger of someone predeceased by a spouse he deeply loved.

As she entertained the idea of dating again, Marti scoured library shelves and bookstores looking for resources focused on widowhood romance. What she found were memoirs by celebrity widows (and an occasional widower). These first-person accounts were interesting and insightful, but barely touched on the ins and outs of new relationships. What she wanted—but couldn't find—was information expressly focused on the romantic realities of widows.

She plunged one night into speed dating, which led to a series of dates with a widower who was nearly as inexperienced as she was. After twenty-eight great years with the same guy, this first dating experience was a wild ride. The blog she had launched to manage her grief when her husband Tom died started to document the rudderless journey of dating again.

Mary, who had been divorced for many years, also found herself in an unfamiliar landscape. There were virtually no resources that looked at relationships through the lens of someone dating a widow or widower. She frequently turned to Marti's blog for insight.

One icy evening during a long and lively dinner conversation at a Detroit restaurant, Marti and Mary talked about the dearth of practical information on widowhood dating. As journalists, their curiosity default was the same: to turn to research and writing when they needed to make sense of things. *Finding Love after Loss: A Relationship Roadmap for Widows* is the result.

Because Marti's blog about her widowhood experiences provided the nexus of ideas for the book project, each chapter ends with a post from her blog, *Life after Widowhood*.

This book plumbs the findings and opinions of scholars, therapists, and professionals, from studies focused on young military widows with children to research papers on the likelihood of remarriage after widowhood. Marti and Mary found rich detail in a massive investigative project that examined seniors' attitudes about love and marriage. They also looked at an array of separate studies that homed in on everything from finances in widowhood to whether "in sickness and in health" still counts. They talked to experts, including relationship counselors.

What they learned was interesting and informative, but the basic questions remained: *How do widows meet new partners? What kind of relationships do they forge together? How do widows manage their complicated feelings about new romance?*

To see how the research applied to real life, Marti and Mary went to the front line and started talking to widows and, sometimes, the people they date. In those interviews, they found candid, painful, and often-defiant tales from the trenches about such intimate subjects as sex with a new partner; the commingling of money; and children, in-laws, and friends who rear up in surprise at the notion that widows might seek new romance. Many of those widows' stories and experiences are detailed in this book. To protect their privacy, real names are not used.

The rich treasure trove of information that began to build was revealing. Many of these widows were making up the game as they went along, often operating under new, even radical, rules of engagement. Marti and Mary talked to people who had both successful and not-so-successful marriages or long-term relationships before widowhood. Some of these women found glorious new love, including—to their shock—partners they loved even more than their first spouses. Some sought less intensive connections, although still rich with affection and companionship. These women were not wired for life alone and they had no wish to settle for that. Some widows even aspired to be serial daters, to have only sex-based relationships, or even to have relationships with people who were already in relationships.

Even more, what started for many widows as a quest for a date and new love turned into a much greater exploration of the fullness of life.

Marti and Mary launched this project with some preconceived ideas, which they quickly had to discard. For starters, they were astonished to learn how many widows (and widowers) there are in this country. One-third of older women in the United States have lost a partner (a statistic that swelled with the COVID-19 pandemic). Also unexpected was how open and explicit these women were in talking about their lives. Many had carved out new romance. If a new partner was not in the picture (or not yet), they had female and male friends and relatives who powered a lively social network. Some of the widows still worked or volunteered. Young widows were busy raising their children. Older widows provided childcare for grandchildren. They traveled. They were rebuilding good lives.

Marti and Mary discovered that sex was a great motivator when it came to widows moving back into the dating world. And e-dating, with its seemingly endless (and growing) list of dating apps, proved the most popular way to meet partners. The widows weren't shy about discussing their online forays, although it was eye-opening to see how hard the scammers targeted them on dating sites. "Cyberstalking," "catfishing," . . . the widows' vocabulary quickly expanded once they began to seek a partner online.

The widow interviews confirmed the importance of shared values in finding a good and enduring match. Values can make or break a relationship, and it doesn't take women long to figure that out. Importantly, the values question goes far beyond common political views or alignment on how clean the house should be. Values—and honesty—underpin a solid and resilient relationship.

It was also a surprise to see how quickly widows worked to realign their dating strategies in the face of the COVID-19 quarantine. Even more, the isolation of the quarantine sparked some who had been on the fence to jump into dating or, if they were already dating, to fast-track the journey so they could create safe "bubbles" with their new love matches. (That fast-tracking had both good and disastrous results.)

Interviews with widows form the foundation of this book and they provided its most illuminating information. But the interview with a high-end, professional matchmaking service wasn't far behind. For widows willing to spend big bucks, a perfect partner is promised.

Meanwhile, from her personal experience, Marti knew how losing a spouse can compromise the body. The interviews with widows reinforced just how often a loved one's death triggers a survivor's illness.

To discuss love and death together is not easy. Widowhood dating is an unusual beast in that it flips the usual pattern: instead of death being the end of the game, it is the beginning of a new story. The goal of this book is to help women understand the way widowhood changes them—and those around them—and the cascading effect that it has on their lives, their aspirations and, importantly, their relationships. It explores the places where traditional marriage and widowhood are congruent and the areas where they butt heads. It looks at what widows trade for love and what they choose over love.

The number of widows in the United States is on the rise. As the pages of *Finding Love after Loss* reveal, this growing demographic is quietly reengineering social connections and redefining romantic relationships in new and unexpected ways. The widows' experiences shared in this book shape a playbook for those who believe love can strike more than once.

• 1 •

Loving Again

*And they do come out of it, that's true. After a year, after five.
But they don't come out of it like a train coming out of a tunnel,
bursting through the downs into sunshine and that swift, rattling
descent to the Channel; they come out of it as a gull comes out of
an oil-slick. They are tarred and feathered for life.*

—Author Julian Barnes on grief, in *Flaubert's Parrot*

Love is one of the most joyous things that anchors the human experience. That's why it's so hard to give up.

In the mosh pit of romance, people scramble to make connections. They touch, they slam, they sweat, they laugh. They plow through energy and pheromones as if both will replenish forever. Tucked among those teeming masses is a group that stands a little apart from the rest. They carry with them different experiences, expectations, and, yes, baggage, than their divorced and never-married counterparts.

They are the nation's widows. As they realize they have years still to live, many are choosing not to live them alone. They rail against the idea of retreating into solitude or settling for platonic friendships. They want to be happy. They want companionship. They want intimacy.

In increasing numbers, they are boldly striking out in search of love again. Along the way, they are discovering just *how* different they are from everyone else in the dating arena.

"Other people just don't get us," said Evie, whose husband died as the couple began an early retirement. Another widow told us that she feared she would look like a bleak figure to potential mates who ran across her profile on dating apps. Other widows said they were surprised

1

to discover how problematic their return to romance proved for friends and families, including in-laws.

Amy, widowed after fifty-one years of marriage, said everything after her husband died—including new romance—left her with the uneasy feeling that she was "flying by the seat of my pants." Still another widow said that each time she went out with a new date, she felt a constant struggle not to compare the man in front of her to her late husband, whom she had deeply loved.

Dating has never been easy. Dating in widowhood is no exception. But widowhood dating can also be breathtaking. Widows who seek new relationships are, in some ways, a lodestar for love. They committed to the union until "death do us part," they held to that oath and, even amid loss, they have not abandoned their belief in love. Each widow's quest for a new relationship teaches that life can tote chest-splitting loss while also celebrating new, buoyant happiness.

Widows longing for romance wake up each day intensely aware of how their lives have capsized. For years, sometimes decades, these women moved, thought, and responded like the spouses or partners that they were. They thrived as co-conspirators in steady, and often predictable, romantic partnerships. Then death came, made them suddenly single, and forced them to remap their interior geographies—often on the fly. They felt lost and sad but also, eventually, a little bit excited about the prospect that they could start anew.

As they acknowledge that happiness doesn't just come knocking at the door, they aren't sure what they need to do to redesign their lives. And they can't find anyone else to tell them, which is remarkable given the sheer number of widows in the United States.

Widows belong to a formidable demographic. More than seven hundred thousand US women experience the death of a life partner each year (a statistic that jumped even higher during the COVID-19 pandemic), and today there are more than eleven million widows in the United States. If they all lived in a single place, it would be nearly one-and-a-half times the size of New York City. And it wouldn't be, as many people might think, a city of old women. The average age of widowhood is only in the mid-fifties.

So many women, and yet their stories unfold so quietly away from the spotlight. Books, blogs, television shows, podcasts, and even movies detail the romantic pathways of men and women, straight and gay (and trans). They plumb the experiences of college students, young adults, divorced individuals, first-time brides, virgins, and people with several marriages already under their belts. Yet widows' stories happen out of sight, almost hidden. How are these women salvaging their lives? How are they envisioning their next chapters? How are they reclaiming love?

The answer is that they are doing it creatively, energetically, and almost covertly, breaking the rules because no one is watching. They are experimenting with new levels of commitment (or none at all), customizing their liaisons, ignoring the well-intentioned advice of friends, and behaving impressively unlike the generations of widows that preceded them. Without a playbook that matches their needs, they are rewriting new and interesting ground rules.

Perhaps more than anyone else seeking romance, today's widows are conscious of time. In part, it is because they are living the repercussions of life's brevity. For older widows, in particular, there is an acknowledgment that their lifespan is not infinite. *Seize the day* is an alluring mantra, as evidenced in the whirlwind romance of an eighty-year-old widow and an eighty-two-year-old widower who found each other on a dating website for Catholics.[1] Three days after they connected online, they met in person. Three days after that, the widower proposed.

Some of their children were taken aback by the speed of the commitment, and the bride-to-be, citing her background in psychology, acknowledged that she normally would have advised someone in her place to take it slower. However, she declared that her certainty was ironclad. The groom-to-be was more practical: "At my age, I can't go slow."

Not all widows, of course, take the fast track to new love. But nearly all widows ponder the big question of whether another love is even possible in widowhood and, if so, how it might look. Luckily for them, the human heart is big enough to encompass more than one romantic love. Many widows, especially in the earliest weeks and months of grief, do not believe that. They can't imagine regaining happiness again, let alone being in a relationship again. Over time, however, holes are punched into the crushing weight of bereavement and lightness starts to filter in.

Women who have pushed ahead in search of love have come to understand that they can carry two relationships—the one they will always have with their deceased partner and the new one that unfolds with the different person they have become. That widows can, do, and should have new partners in their lives is a testimony to the complex pull of romantic love.

Still, these romantic journeys are not without challenges. As widows jettison into the tumultuous world of romance, they find a dating scene that is daunting. It has been years (perhaps decades) since they last dabbled in this playground, and the new rules are dizzying. They've heard horror stories about online matches as well as warnings about internet scams targeting widows. Their children or extended families may be throwing wrenches into their plans for romance.

At the same time, they may be juggling illogical guilt feelings and grief triggers. Their health may be under duress. They may fear that a new romance will disrupt their financial situation or carry them back to caregiving, a place they've been and don't want to return. They have angst about getting naked with someone new, worry whether some values are negotiable, and work to identify their deal busters.

Research on widowhood romance is not abundant, but there are some surveys, studies, and statistics that help tell the story of today's widows and their yearning for a second chapter. One, the Legacy Project, is a survey of twelve hundred people ages sixty-five and older in the United States. Anchored by detailed interviews with open-ended questions, this project compiled advice for living better, happier lives. Among the things couples in the project singled out as must-haves for enduring love were "fidelity, honesty, caring, and humor."[2]

Another source of rich research is the National Marriage Project, an initiative at the University of Virginia that tracks how marriages are made and maintained and what that means for the United States.[3] We looked at these—and many other—studies while writing this book. We also interviewed professionals in the field, including dating counselors and a professional matchmaker. Their input helped us better understand the experiences of widowhood dating. But the best advice, the wisest counsel, and the smartest coaching came from widows themselves.

We interviewed widows who had both successful and not-so-successful marriages. There were widows who remarried and those who decided to cohabitate with new partners. There were widows who merged their families with those of their new lovers and those who kept everyone apart. One widow was happier with her new romantic partner than she had been with her husband, and there was a septuagenarian who surprised herself by entering a polyamorous relationship. There were many widows who ditched the traditional "for richer and poorer, in sickness and in health" vows the second time around.

This isn't your grandmother's widowhood scene, not by a long shot.

The stories of widows who build new romances are inspirational and challenging. These are the women who, separated by death from the partners they loved, have gathered up their reservoir of resilience to write a new love story. Along the way, they are rejiggering the ways they think about love and relationships in all its permutations—from flings, affairs, and friends-with-benefits to deep and fulfilling new marriages or commitments.

Why do these widows' stories matter? Because they have *lived the experiences*. They also matter because, cumulatively, they show how one of the largest generations in our nation's history is reengineering our social connections and relationships. They are disrupters. In many ways, they are also heretics, ditching the old rules and replacing them with new and creative alternatives.

Evie's right. People don't always understand widows. Death reshapes those left behind, and this recalibration—still-in-progress—can be confounding for the new romantic partners. For them, it may seem akin to following Google Maps instructions while road construction is underway. Delays, detours, traffic jams, extra time to reach a destination, and scenery that may be far different (although often lovelier) than expected.

This book busts the myths about dating in widowhood, details the real-life romances of those who have shaped new relationships, looks at common obstacles for people reentering the dating arena (*What about the in-laws?*), and reveals the unconventional ways widows are merging their lives with new partners. It offers a primer for online dating, the big game-changer on the romance scene. It even explores pandemic dating.

This is a book about love, lost and found. It is a salute to women who continue to believe in love, in second chances, in the power of connection.

FROM MARTI'S BLOG

(Marti's husband, Tom, died of terminal brain cancer on February 15, 2012. He was fifty-eight. Marti's blog documents her thoughts and experiences in the years that followed.)

A Sweet Missive on New Year's Eve

This year, I spent New Year's Eve at my friend's bar—a music club in the city. It's a comfortable place to hang out with friendly bartenders, a great micro-brew selection, quality food, and live music almost every night of the week.

My husband Tom and his buddies, during their boys' nights out, always ended their evenings at this Irish pub with roots that go back to the late 1800s. That ritual, at least Tom's role in it, ended with his death.

This year, some of my friends were going to sporting events or dinner but said they would drop by the bar before the midnight toast. They arrived about eleven, shortly after I got there, and the rhythm of the place, which attracts a young crowd, was stepping up its pace. Patrons began ordering fresh beers and shots—Jameson, Jack, Fireballs, tequila.

Right before midnight, my friend George, who was my husband's closest friend, and his wife wanted me to come look at the bar top. This was not totally a surprise because I saw George earlier in the week, and he told me he had something to show me next time we were at the bar.

The bar top at this place is interesting. Roughly eight years ago, the owner decided he wanted to layer it with a variety of guitar picks. Many of them had sayings or initials or designs done by friends and customers. Some picks had professional logos; others were blank but colorful. After gathering the picks, he had his friends (Tom included) glue them randomly to the top of the bar. A layer of shellac was applied over them to give the top a waterproof but artful, music-oriented surface.

I vaguely remember hearing about this effort because the owner was upset that the shellac smeared what was written on many of the picks. Regardless, I thought it was a great idea, and it still looks quite good.

Back to New Year's Eve. As I walked over to George and his wife with their phone flashlights illuminating the bar top, I was told to look carefully. There, among dozens of colorful picks, was a pearl-colored one. In black handwriting I know so well it read "Tom loves Marti." Midnight struck and my friends gave me a hug.

I got a little teary but not overly emotional. A couple years ago seeing this would have made me sad and, no doubt, set off a swell of tears. That night, it made me feel good and reminded me that someone loved me a lot for many years. I'd sat at that bar probably a dozen times since Tom's death, never knowing there was a little, personal missive to me. Thanks, Tom, for the reminder. And thanks, my friends, for waiting to show me. It was a good way to start the new year.

• 2 •

Busting the Myths

What I am begins to be revealed now that I am alone. In such revelation is terror.

—Author Joyce Carol Oates, in *A Widow's Story*

There is a saying: *There's nothing stronger than a woman who has rebuilt herself.* For widows, new love can be an important part of that transformation.

Widows may find themselves exhilarated about the prospect of romance again. They feel capable of sharing their lives anew, willing to take the steps required to seek love after loss, ready to transform. While that process is underway, however, widows are keenly aware of the chinks in their armor. They've been through a lot and may hesitate about exposing themselves. They feel scared, vulnerable, afraid of more abandonment. They are sad—that goes without saying—and angered and frustrated by days when the grief can't be reeled in.

Against their own whirling emotions, they are confronted—and confused—by the many, many myths of widowhood. These are the contradictory beliefs, the advice, and the adages that continue to circulate. There is an impressive number of them, each more absurd than the next. We have identified the Top Ten.

Every widow contemplating the pursuit of new romance should understand these myths. And bust them.

MYTH NO. 1: WIDOWS ARE FRAGILE AND VULNERABLE.

At a Washington, DC, dinner party, a guest—who happened to be a social worker—struck up a conversation with a woman in a new relationship with a widower. "Oh, I never date widowers," the social worker confided. "You can't ever leave them. It's about them being abandoned all over again."

Death changes a person's existence in a flash. Suddenly a woman realizes the future she had with her partner, the life they envisioned, has evaporated. The safety net, the security a woman felt with a spouse at her side, is gone. That concrete footing is transformed into sand or, worse, quicksand. It is hard to imagine a more stressful life event than the death of a spouse or long-time mate.

But most widows, including older adults who were in enduring and happy marriages, are wired for resilience. The first months are hard and may be marked by health setbacks and depression. But widows tend to spring back, physically and mentally, and sometimes sooner than people expect. Human beings have an amazing capacity to adapt to stressful events.

Nonetheless, the idea of the vulnerability of widows is still floating out there in the public sphere. In previous generations, women were even expected to roam around wearing black—or, at least, black armbands—so people would have a visual reminder to treat them gingerly. That runs counter to the realization that widowhood, despite its awfulness, can toughen women. Wives who ended up caring for a dying spouse, for example, often feel stronger once that burden has been taken from them. After their initial daunting period of bereavement, they may have more energy than they did while caregiving and more time to take care of themselves. They bristle at those who treat them protectively.

"It was a real eye-opener for me that I had all this inner strength," said Amy, who had been married fifty-one years when her husband died. "I don't worry about who will take care of me." She dated several men after her husband died and declined to pursue a relationship when she sensed a man wanted to defend or shield her.

The thing about widowhood is that women do not heal from the loss of a spouse. Rather, they adapt to their reality.

Who wants to launch a romance with someone who might shatter? No one—or certainly no one with a healthy take on relationships.

That's why widows need to own their strength and tenacity. They are not helpless, and they do not need to be an object of care. They are re-creating themselves, becoming empowered, and the very act of seeking love again is a sign they have Goliath-like strength.

MYTH NO. 2: GRIEF EVENTUALLY GOES AWAY.

In his book *Benedictus*, a collection of poetic blessings, John O'Donohue writes of

> Days when you have your heart back,
> You are able to function well
> Until in the middle of work or encounter,
> Suddenly with no warning,
> You are ambushed by grief.

People who date a widow may assume that the bereavement pro-cess eventually comes to an end. But grief has no shelf life. It gets easier to manage with time. Its sharp edges soften. In fact, being in a new relationship may hasten that process, but it doesn't delete grief.

As any widow knows, grief can resurface at any time, in any place. An anniversary date, a birthday that won't be celebrated, a favorite song of a now-deceased partner, or a place that had special emotional impor-tance. All can trigger the sudden return of sorrow. Even walking past a stranger in a familiar cologne can bring on a grief attack, as can spotting someone biking in the distance who resembles an absent husband, wife, or partner.

"I don't drive by the hospital where he died. I go two blocks south," said Evie, who was married thirty-seven years when her hus-band died unexpectedly. "I don't listen to music anymore. That was something we shared—he was a big music person. He was also a huge basketball fan and I still haven't watched a game since his death. And that's six years now."

As widows know, grief flashbacks are like menopausal hot flashes: they can't be predicted and they can't be suppressed. Some widows may find themselves repeatedly slammed back to the same visceral sorrow as the first days of their bereavement. At these moments, new partners may have to dig deep into their empathy bags. Holidays can be especially difficult.

When a widow dates again—or even remarries—her previous life does not evaporate. What's important to remember is, despite the pain, grief attacks are a normal, maybe even a healthy, part of the bereavement journey. Widows can give the trigger moments the respect they merit, for in many ways they pay testimony to how deeply anchored the lost relationship is. Widows can also learn to reframe grief attacks so the recollections are less painful.

The new romantic partners of widows, meanwhile, must accept that grief episodes are part of the package. They may find it helpful to note significant dates—anniversaries, birthdays—on a calendar so they aren't caught off guard. They might also encourage the widows in their life to talk about the pain of the moment (although widows need to remember that the people they date are not their therapists).

Some people emerge from grief faster, sturdier, than others. Although too many widows torture themselves wondering if "enough" time has passed before dating, there is no time rule. A widow steps forward toward new love when she is ready. If she is dating and finds that grief attacks come too frequently, too intensely, bringing too much disruption or too much alienation, she might think about retreating from the romance scene for a minute. Maybe therapy is in order.

However, the idea that grief will cease is a fairy tale.

MYTH NO. 3: WIDOWS WILL ONLY FIND SUCCESSFUL LOVE WITH SOMEONE WHO ALSO LOST A PARTNER.

Nearly every widow we interviewed for this book had one requirement when they began their quest for a new lover: that he (or she) also be widowed. Women who feel ready to date after a partner dies assume that only someone else who has experienced a deep loss can understand what they have been through.

Trudy, a widow for ten years, was determined to only fall in love with a widower. For a moment, she thought she'd found him. "[He was] a very nice widower who had been married for thirty years. He was sweet, but he was very brokenhearted," she said. "He wasn't really ready for a relationship, so it never worked out."

She later found happy, solid love with a twice-divorced man.

Detroit-area executive Jack was in his late forties when his wife died of cancer, leaving him alone with their three young children. Marriage marked the happiest stretch of his life, and he was crystal clear about his desire to remarry. Like Trudy, he felt his best match would be with someone who had also lost a spouse. However, a widower friend warned Jack that if he only dated widows, he would be single forever. "Still, I thought widows and widowers were on higher ground than everybody else," Jack admitted. "We made great life decisions on choosing a partner, and they were torn away from us. When you meet another widow, it immediately creates a strong connection. You have a shared experience."

After four years of dating that went nowhere, Jack began a successful relationship with a divorced woman with children younger than his.

At the beginning of their dating journey, most widows think they must stick with their kind. They steer clear of divorced daters and never-marrieds. However, it doesn't take long for them to slam into a practicality that even love can't override. The insular all-widowed dating pool is just too small.

The number of widows in the world vastly outweighs the number of widowers. It's simple math: women live longer than men, and many marry men older than them. Biology may play a role in men's shorter lifespans, but a portion of this imbalance comes from men's exposure to risk. They disproportionately populate the military forces, including combat units. Many are employed in dangerous jobs. They pursue different kinds of thrills than women. During the 2020 pandemic, they were less likely than women to survive a complicated case of COVID-19.

Certainly, it's not impossible to pair up with someone else who is widowed. We found several widows who did just that with happy results. But widows who limit their dating pool are working against the odds and making their journey to new romance more difficult than it needs to be. Widows do best when they toss their hat into a ring that is big and wide and filled with people who share their interests and values, who may live in their same town or city.

We also ran into women who intentionally strive to date people who are *not* widowed. "If I'm choosing the kind of person I might date next, if they're a widower, I think twice again," one widow said.

"I guess the question is: Do you want to go with someone fresh who doesn't have a history involving grief?"

MYTH NO. 4: FRIENDS AND FAMILY KNOW WHAT'S BEST FOR A WIDOW.

People close to a widow can provide an anchor in bereavement. These friends and family members can be a widow's rock—until, that is, the widow decides to pursue a new relationship. Many widows have friends and family who support their search for new love. But not all. And that pushback can be difficult, eroding friendships and weighing heavily on happiness. It is a predicament particular to widowhood dating, and people often are not shy about how they feel with blunt comments such as:

It's too soon to date.
How will your in-laws feel?
Your children need your full attention now.
It's not healthy for your children to see you in another relationship.
Won't you dishonor your husband's memory if you remarry?
You need to take more time or it will look like you didn't love
    your spouse enough.

Divorced women and others whose relationships have ended do not hesitate to begin new ones. Not widows. They stand apart, often wracked with complex feelings that can be inflamed even more by interfering friends and family.

Widows don't want to give up intimacy or companionship. A widow knows her spouse is never returning. Yet even when she acknowledges that she has the right to happiness again, she hears people close to her opposing that choice, marginalizing her.

Gretchen found her family shocked by the notion she would date again. Her husband died at age fifty-nine after a decade-long illness. "They all seemed to think that I should be by myself for a number of years before I date," Gretchen said. "My granddaughter, especially, had a very difficult time with it. But I had my life to live.

"Anyway, even though I started dating only a year after my husband's death," she said, "I had been living with his illness and inevitable death for ten years."

Doug, a widower, faced similar pushback. "For six months I was dazed and confused. My grief was extreme at that time, and I joined a support group. But then I came out of it," Doug said. "I told my friends and family I'm looking for romance again. My sister-in-law was opposed to me dating. My mother-in-law, my father-in-law, everybody was against me dating."

His children were uncomfortable when he briefly moved in with a woman he dated. "They said, 'Everything's too fast, Dad. You've got to slow down,'" Doug recalled. "But I'm very conscious of age. I'm seventy years old and I feel like there's an expiration date for this whole process, that I'll reach a point where I can't date anymore."

There are a lot of hurtful things (often unintentional) that can interfere with widows moving forward. Being judged is one of them—especially by people who have never been through the experience. Restarting a romantic life is already awkward. Widows don't necessarily want to hide that they are open to a new relationship, but it can feel embarrassing and, yes, at times disloyal. Even if they are confident their spouse would have wanted them to go out and find happiness, friends may struggle with that idea. Their world, too, has been tossed and they may feel—consciously or subconsciously—that the widow is trying to remake it with new people.

Most disconcerting may be the family's reaction. If there are children (especially older children), a widow may worry that her new search for love will cause greater disruption to her already-unsettled family. A widow's siblings may want her to take more time to "recover." And what about her in-laws? If she's lucky, they will be understanding. If she's not lucky, they will see her dating as an affront. This is treacherous territory, and a widow has to tread carefully to keep the peace while also respecting her own needs.

Widows have to listen to their hearts, gauge their readiness to date, and then trust their decisions. They are not trying to replace or re-create what they have lost. They are embarking on a new, different, loving relationship that in no way changes or diminishes the previous one. Friends and family should be invited to support that choice, but never to hinder it.

MYTH NO. 5: WIDOWS WANT TO REMARRY.

"Everybody in my family thought I was going to get married right away," said Barbé, widowed thirteen years ago. "This is the first time I've been alone in my life and I am enjoying the independence I've gained through widowhood." She dates but she has no interest in marriage.

People seem to think widows, naturally, will remarry given the opportunity. Those who like to wager might be pushing the odds if they gave that assumption more than a fifty-fifty chance.

A 2014 study by the Pew Research Center found that most people who have been married want the formality of marriage again.[1] However, once widows and other women hit age sixty-five, that tendency drops dramatically to only 40 percent—less than any other widowed age group, except for the small eighteen-to-thirty-four-year-old segment.

Of course, many widows (and even more widowers) desire to remarry. They want again something close to what they used to have, something familiar. The problem comes when people *assume* that remarriage is why a widow is dating again.

Maura, a divorced woman seeking new love as she neared retirement, was elated when a widower showed interest in her. She had aspired to date a widower. Her reasoning? Widowers (and in her estimation, widows, too) know how to make a marriage work. And if they married once, they would want to commit long term again.

"He will tell me many touching stories about his wife, and I like to hear them. You feel like you were there and that you would love her, too," Maura said of her widower. "When people are able to talk about someone with great love, then you know they are capable of love." Maura stayed involved with this man for a while but, to her disappointment, they never discussed marriage. They ended their romantic relationship but remain friends.

When broken down by gender, almost two-thirds of men remarry. (In many ways, Maura was on the right track.) Not so with widows. Several widows we interviewed—even the ones who had been in long and happy marriages—told us that remarriage wasn't their goal. In its place, they had devised unexpected and creative ways to shape their new relationships, from cohabiting full time to living together on certain days of the week. For them, to love again did not necessarily translate into a legal commitment. In fact, their customized family and living arrangements made the transition to a new relationship feel easier and safer.

MYTH NO. 6: DIVORCED AND WIDOWED PEOPLE HAVE SOMETHING IN COMMON.

A divorcee had harsh words about this book. "Who is it for? How is it different than books about divorced people dating? Both people are single. I don't see the difference."

Yes, widows and divorced people have both seen a marriage come to an end. However, these two groups have not traveled the same road. In fact, the greatest *difference* between the divorced and the widowed is experiential. Widows talk about the temptation to commit great bodily harm when divorced people claim that they "understand how you feel."

Widows go through a gut-ripping process that is alien to everyone else. Not only does it change their day-to-day circumstances, but it changes their very life in unexpected ways. The people who survive the death of a spouse or significant other are not the same people they were before. Part of bereavement is the process of acknowledging that a widow has emerged as a new person on a new path.

The *HuffPost* has gone so far as to characterize the death versus divorce dichotomy as the dating world's "Epic Struggle," akin to other classic conflicts: "David vs. Goliath; the Hatfields vs. the McCoys; Billie Jean vs. Bobby Riggs; the Beatles vs. the Rolling Stones; Ginger vs. Mary Ann."[2]

That's not to say divorce is easy. Or that it doesn't transform people. But in many cases, divorce brings a person's worst nightmare to an end. When death touches a marriage, on the other hand, the worst nightmare may be just beginning. People divorce because their marriages are *not* happy. A marriage that erodes into divorce may piggyback on animosity, especially if the split is marked by a legal brawl or custody battle. Many widows have never experienced that type of broken trust. In fact, they dread divorced daters who are angry about their exes or who show interest then shy away when it comes to a long-haul commitment.

For divorced people, meanwhile, getting *beyond* a first marriage is often a healthy goal. They may be unaccustomed to dating people who effusively praise a former spouse. Divorced people may also notice that the losses experienced by widows are met with public compassion while theirs are not. "Telling a guy you just met that you are a widow immediately elicits an 'I'm sorry,'" said Trudy. "I always say, 'It's not your fault.'"

These gaps in experience are not insurmountable for those willing to take a stab at love, to push their empathy boundaries, to raise patience to an art form. Widows may find it helpful to talk about what they have been through. They should encourage the people they are dating to ask questions. Since love is a two-way venture, widows should also be willing to listen to and try to understand the relationship struggles of the people across the table from them, whether divorced or not.

MYTH NO. 7: BEWARE OF PARTNERING WITH DIVORCED PEOPLE—THEY WON'T STICK WITH THE COMMITMENT.

Here they are again, those divorced people. This time widows are the ones toting the misconceptions. They fear that re-partnering with a divorced person may be too risky. *Did they divorce because they did something, such as cheating, that harmed the relationship? Did they give up on love too soon? What if they go back to their former spouse?*

A widow talked to us about dating a divorced man. "I had been in a forty-year marriage, and I had a little bit of a concern because he was divorced," she said. "I was afraid the divorce meant he hadn't put in the effort or that he had screwed up." Once she stepped away from that stereotype, their relationship was able to flourish.

"I've come to understand that people do grow apart, and that divorce does not necessarily equal failure," she said.

Jack, a widower, has been with his girlfriend for more than five years now. They talk about getting engaged, but he hasn't hit the "100 percent sure" mark yet, largely because she is divorced. For him, a secure romance is anchored in marriage. He worries she might one day decide to return to her ex-husband.

Many widows are most comfortable thinking of marriage in absolute terms. They may feel divorce reflects a negotiable connection to permanent coupling, the idea that marriage is an option but not the only option. At the same time, the romantic journeys of divorced people may be marked by a caution that confuses widows who frame commitment as a happy goal. Truth told, divorce—like all romance—comes in a long menu of flavors. Certainly, some divorces are messy, but not all. To assume that divorce translates into a lack of commitment to a long-term romance is short-sighted and self-defeating.

Love is an extraordinary human experience, delicate, terrifying, transcendent—and hard to resist. A new romance, any new relationship, necessarily accommodates the experiences of both partners. But it also begins from ground zero. What happened before is not the template for what will happen again.

MYTH NO. 8: THERE IS A STANDARD TIME FOR BEREAVEMENT AND TO SHOW RESPECT THAT SHOULD PASS BEFORE WIDOWHOOD DATING BEGINS.

Says who?

There seems to be a random calendar that people expect widows to follow. At least a year, or even two, should pass before they even consider dating again. (For widowers, interestingly, friends and family tend to be more forgiving on this point, often putting a year as the adequate standard.) As a corollary, a widow should go out on three dates before discussing any serious medical problems that need to be shared and at least three dates before having sex. Three! The magic number for widowhood dating.

The insistence on having vibrant women sitting at home in black mourning clothes because of random calendar requirements has gone the way of newspaper dating ads. The scheduling police seem oblivious to the fact that every widow's loss, every widow's bereavement, is hers alone. Some women undergo a long period at a deteriorating loved one's bedside, slowly reconciling to the inevitable. They may begin to move through the stages of grief even before a spouse or partner has died. Older widows, meanwhile, may feel the pressure of time: *I'm not getting any younger and I won't live forever.* Some women may have lived through less-than-happy marriages, anxious for a chance at the great love that eluded them.

There's also the bizarre idea that if a widow is dating, she's "over" her grief. Even a new love doesn't take that away. Grief can coexist with love. Widows care about what their friends say and disapproval or judgment can sting even more when the widows are emotionally weakened by grief. Sure, sometimes widows step out into the dating world too soon then have to backtrack. But that's OK. They are simply following the universal urge to connect with another human in a meaningful way.

MYTH NO. 9: WIDOWS ARE TOO OLD TO DATE.

The average age of a widow in the United States is only fifty-nine, according to the US Census Bureau. The National Center for Health Statistics, meanwhile, put the average lifespan of a woman in the United States at eighty-one years old.[3] That means the "average" widow still has more than two decades to invest in a lovely, caring romance. That's twice as long as a typical first marriage lasts in the United States.[4]

Even if widowhood only touched the oldest of our citizens, that doesn't make them any less date-worthy. What the too-old-to-date myth reflects is an ingrained and careless—even callous—disregard for widows as full human beings. Studies find that friends rarely offer widows an introduction to a single friend. Widows are routinely left out of social gatherings, the invisible people in the room. Once they are no longer part of a couple, they are even dropped from the invitations of friends (particularly when the other guests are couples).

Scholar Amanda Barusch, whose research focuses on the experiences of older adults, has found that older women—including widows—are even left out of studies about relationships. Research on marriage, for example, is three times more likely to focus on younger adults than on seniors.[5]

When naysayers discount widows as romance-eligible, they are excluding a significant part of the population. Nearly 40 percent of women over sixty-five in the United States are widows. Among Black women, more than 46 percent of older women are widowed, according to the *Who Are Americans 65 and Older?* report from the US Census.[6]

For this book, we tracked the stories of widows who remarried even into their nineties. People who use ageism as a reason to discourage widows from dating are stuck in the past. In many ways, older widows are especially primed for new relationships because they carry two critical notions: that good companionship is important and that time is limited.

MYTH NO. 10: A WIDOW IS A WIDOW IS A WIDOW (WITH APOLOGIES TO GERTRUDE STEIN).

People think of widows as a homogenous demographic. Wrong. They are as diverse as the population as a whole. Bereavement doesn't give them anything in common except loss.

The most significant variable is age. Young widows face many different experiences than older widows. About 16 percent of all widows fall into the "younger widow" category, which studies generally categorize as between the ages of eighteen and fifty-five.

A younger widow is more likely to be raising children, working, or both, which means the death of her spouse sparked a greater upheaval in her day-to-day life than did the death of an older woman's partner. Since a younger widow's spouse is more likely to have died unexpectedly, she has had no time to prepare in any way for loss. Younger widows may be left in more tenuous financial straits than older widows, and they may face more pronounced health consequences.[7]

Services and resources set up to help widows are designed for older women; older women are more likely to know other widows. That gap slows younger widows' adjustment after their lives have been derailed.

Theresa, a mother of three, was widowed at forty-four. Her husband died of a sudden heart attack the day after he passed a physical exam to start a new job. "After he died, I remember thinking, 'I can't believe we had him get a vasectomy. Here I am, and I'll have to worry about pregnancy again if I meet someone.' Birth control. That's not one of the things they talk about when you start reading about widowhood."

Other younger widows said they felt uncomfortable talking about their marital status around people their age. One widower, who was in his thirties when his wife died, said he didn't tell his dates that he was a widower until they had gone out a few times. "I thought it would have some type of negative impact on my dealings with women," he said.

Meg was widowed at forty-five. It was while attending weddings that she realized she had been, as she put it, "reclassified."

"Instead of being seated with all my friends who are couples, I was put at the widows and gays tables. I had no idea that this table even existed, that the herd separated itself out," she said. "Even when my own parents were at the same wedding, I was separated out and seated away from them."

Since younger widows' friends tend to be young themselves, and less experienced with death, they often make tone-deaf comments about death, leaving widows feeling disconnected from their social groups. Meg said she was appalled when the husband of a friend made a pass early in her widowhood. Theresa said widowhood made her an outsider among her friends.

"When you're a certain age—at seventy-five or eighty—and you're a widow, that seems almost normal to people. You probably have friends who are widows," Theresa said. "But for me, among people my own age, I'm always the only widow, the one who is different."

These distinctions can make dating for younger widows more complex.

Loving after loss is complicated, regardless of age. Baseless myths are no help.

FROM MARTI'S BLOG

Don't Be Fooled. Grieving Isn't Over in a Year.

About a year after Tom died, I felt a bit of relief from grieving. It was my goal to get through that first year, thinking I'd feel better afterward. Well, I felt the weight of the sadness lift and, shortly after, embarked on a few adventures out of my comfort zone.

Initially, this felt good, and I figured I was over the worst of it. But I began to hear from widow/widowers and read that the second year can be harder than the first. I dismissed this thinking because I thought I was tougher than most.

Meanwhile, I started having negative experiences—unsettling moments with guys and dating, a looming layoff at my job, and unexpected problems on the health front. With each setback, I started grieving again. I was back to crying and, even though active socially, I just felt really glum a lot. My revelation? The second year of grieving can, indeed, be harder than the first.

Why? It becomes harshly real that your loved one is dead—gone for good. You see your married friends together enjoying travel, parties, nights out with other couples, and you aren't part of that. You see your couple friends taking care of each other, and realize you have no one to protect you anymore—but you.

So, yes, don't fool yourself that if you tough out that first year, it will be better than the second year. I've now started my third year as a widow, and I think I may have weathered the eye of the storm. I still cry and have my moments, but I'm thinking about other things. I'm not obsessing as much anymore. My concerns are more focused on what I'm doing this weekend for fun, who is available to go out with me, and the well-being of my friends and family.

• 3 •

Santa Sent Me a Man

You know, the man of my dreams might walk round the corner tomorrow. I'm older and wiser and I think I'd make a great girl-friend. I live in the realm of romantic possibility.

—Stevie Nicks, singer and songwriter

Susanna grieved for two years and wasn't consciously thinking about a new relationship until the man dressed as Santa at her church holiday party surprised her with a question. "What do you want for Christmas?"

Susanna's marriage was a blended one. She described it as "yours, mine, ours." Both she and her spouse had children before they met, and they merged their families to form a clan of nine. The marriage was in its twelfth year when illness struck. Six years later, at age fifty-six, Susanna had a new identity: widow.

Now, at this holiday party, Santa was waiting for the widow's wish list. "I told him I wanted a widower who had his act together, who had been widowed at least two years ago, and who was interested in a relationship," Susanna said. "Santa passed me a phone number. He said, 'It isn't exactly what you're looking for but why don't you give it a try?'"

She made what she described as "a very cold call," discovering that Santa hadn't given the voice on the other end of the phone any advance notice. Still, the man was willing to meet. He and Susanna got together for breakfast. And then for a movie. And then for a play, all the while enjoying each other's company. "He wasn't a widower, he was divorced, but he asked if we could try dating for a little while and just see how things worked out," Susanna said. Their relationship lasted four years.

23

How *do* widows find new mates?

Dame Judi Dench, who was widowed in 2001 after thirty years of marriage, has been in a relationship for several years with a conservationist who invited her to unveil an exhibit at her neighborhood nature center.[1] Retired public radio host Diane Rehm found new love and remarriage with John Hagedorn, a Lutheran minister she first met twenty-eight years earlier at the wedding of a mutual friend's daughter. When Hagedorn heard that Rehm's husband had died, he got in touch.[2] And widow Gertrude Mokotoff met widower Alvin Mann at a gym in Middletown, New York, where they both worked out twice a week. Soon after they started dating, he popped the question and she said "yes." Gertrude was ninety-eight and Alvin was ninety-four. They had two delightful years together before Gertrude, a small-city mayor, died.[3]

The pathways to new relationships are many. Even as the COVID-19 pandemic restricted face-to-face dating, it engendered technology to open new ways of connecting. Still, it's not easy for widows to step back into the dating world no matter how they do it. Expectations may be thwarted. The emotional exposure can feel raw. The romance landscape may feel at times more exasperating than exhilarating. In other words, it feels like dating has always felt: a crapshoot.

Debbie met a "very nice guy" while taking her elderly father to a church function. Trudy, a widow for ten years, said starting a relationship after her husband died of cancer wasn't difficult at all. "It seemed like fate in a way. I met a man at the library I frequented and we talked about cancer, loss, et cetera," Trudy said. "He was healing from the loss of his twin brother, and I was recovering from my loss. We helped each other heal. If it had been different circumstances, our paths may not have crossed. We always said, 'We were the shelter for each other.'"

Louise's foray into dating, after her husband's fatal accident ended a four-decade-long marriage, felt like déjà vu. She fell madly in love again with a boyfriend from her long-ago past after they met again at a dinner party hosted by mutual friends. She discovered that he was divorced; he learned she was a widow. "Neither of us had been looking for romance. It just happened," she said.

Another widow, after much unsuccessful matchmaking by her friends, also reconnected with a past romantic partner. Except that this man was married. They began a relationship that went on for ten years—he never divorced—until she ended it.

There are also many stories of people who gear themselves up and head back into the dating jungle only to get a new friend out of the deal rather than a romantic partner. Still, every new friend can lead to more new friends. There's really only one sure-fire way to know if love can be kindled again: strike the match.

START WITH AN OLD-SCHOOL MEETING

Once a widow decides she wants to step into the dating world, she may first meet someone through a friend, a coworker, a neighbor, or a relative. "Once you make that decision to date, and it's not a small decision to make, widows tend to do better by getting recommendations from the people they know and trust," said Marilyn Mendoza, a clinical instructor in the psychiatry department at Tulane University Medical Center.

Another safe avenue for meeting new people, Mendoza said, is by joining a group that regularly rides bikes, plays tennis, enjoys pickleball, or organizes any number of other activities. As for online dating, she recommended considerable prudence. "There's a lot of frustration with online dating. But you can do it as long as you are cautious," she said.

To move back into dating, widows have to be open to the idea of dating, and that means stepping out of their comfort zone. It's not easy. Loneliness can push them. So can lust. Widows with a strong circle of support may get a nudge from friends and family.

"I was testing the water. I had posted a profile on dating sites online but didn't respond to anyone who showed interest. I worried that I wasn't quite ready yet," said Monica, whose partner of nearly two decades died after a difficult year of health struggles. "My daughter was finally the one who told me to go ahead and do it."

Isabella, meanwhile, was a couple of years into widowhood after a forty-year marriage, when she attended a wedding. A young woman she knew came up to compliment her dress. "She told me, 'Oh, Isabella, you look so fuckable,' and I laughed. It sounded so silly. Then I thought, maybe I'd better do something about that. Suddenly I realized it was time."

For some women, the decision to return to dating comes in a snap. A widow wakes up and decides this is the day. For others, a great deal of soul-searching goes on first. They feel the need to sort out complex feelings about whether dating and new love will make them vulnerable to loss again and, if so, whether they can face that reality. Especially if they are younger widows, they have to take into account their children's grief journey. More than anything, women have to understand who they have become as they walk through the wall of bereavement over to the other side.

Women can forfeit a bit of their identity in a marriage. Even for women who have maintained a large degree of independence while married, there is still a transformation that comes with a partner's death. It is not about a widow finding herself—she isn't lost. But she has to put herself in the position to remember who she was before and how to let her core self rise to the surface.

Some widows begin the reclamation process by pursuing enjoyable activities. This can serve the dual purpose of also putting them into social situations that might lead to romance. One widow, to her surprise, met a new beau at a folk-dancing class. Another met a man while in an informal kayaking coterie. Others put their bets on MeetUp, a socializing website that brings groups of people together for activities based on common interests. Taking on a volunteer job at a local museum or theater can be a way to meet romantic partners. Old sparks have been rekindled at class reunions.

Of course, it doesn't always come from planned activities. Sometimes it just happens. One widow we interviewed, Gretchen, was examining the green beans in a grocery store in the little town where her family had a summer cottage when a man stepped over to ask if she would help him select some flowers. It didn't take long for them to become an item.

A sweet story out of England detailed how a woman turned to knitting to help her through her grief after her husband died of cancer in his late forties. Clare's knitting for a charity art project drew the attention of a local TV station. A widower watching the news story decided to give Clare the stash of wool that his wife, also a knitter, had amassed before she died. When Clare went to pick up the donation, the two struck up a wide-ranging conversation and then kept in touch by texts over the weeks that followed. "After months of darkness, I felt warmth and a light shining on me," the man said. After a courtship, they moved in together.[4]

There is also the fascinating story of the two bestselling authors, dying of cancer, whose bereaved spouses fell in love with one another. Lucy Kalanithi, a physician, is the widow of neurosurgeon Paul Kalanithi who wrote *When Breath Becomes Air* before dying of lung cancer in 2015 at age thirty-seven. Lucy moved into the public eye with her TED Talk, "What Makes Life Worth Living in the Face of Death?" It offered advice on how to remain sane while grieving. Nina Riggs, meanwhile, wrote *The Bright Hour: A Memoir of Living and Dying*, which was published just after her death at age thirty-nine. Her husband, John Duberstein, reached out to Lucy Kalanithi. Lucy and John fell head over heels.

GET A STRATEGY

Widows may find a slew of articles and blogs recommending that they buy new clothes, get in shape, or acquire a new hairstyle before they step out. Widows are in the bull's eye for makeover admonitions, largely because women in general are repeatedly told to change themselves to be more appealing. A new dress, some splashy jewelry, or an edgier haircut can embolden widows, but none of those things are mandatory before returning to the dating scene. If they aren't careful, some widows even find pre-dating prep becomes an excuse for not taking the plunge.

A widow venturing back into dating needs to remember that she has to be an active participant, mustering up the courage to take the initiative. Often widows need to push themselves to talk to people. They have to commit to being social, not necessarily because it could lead to a date, but because it's just a healthy thing to do.

Strategies for dating run the gamut from jumping online with a profile picture one daring night to striking up a conversation with an attractive man or woman over kale or Brussels sprouts at the local farmers market. If a widow is lucky, a friend might introduce her to a worthy prospect. For some people, nondating environments—hobby groups, book clubs, sports activities, movie clubs, a glass of wine with a single neighbor—lead from friendship to friendship-with-benefits. Or even more.

Many people assume internet dating apps are the first place to head, but online dating does not have to be the alternative to in-person dating.

Both can be used. In truth, dating apps are simply the prelude to real, in-person dates.

Widows might also consider getting professional help, especially if money doesn't matter. Dating coaches are one option. Rather than face-to-face matchmaking, they counsel and guide people who are seeking matches through online dating sites or provide advice for people trying other options for meeting new mates. Dating coaches cost more than online dating sites (some of which are free) and often include required workshops, homework, or both. Some are fixed commitments—five sessions of advice for $2,500, for example—while others can be long term. Confidence building, combined with a sprinkling of tactical advice, often sits at the foundation of these services. A dating coach can teach widows how to tame their emotions so they don't act (or overreact) on them. They can guide them on how to stay in the middle spectrum between "clingy" and "aloof" while dating and, generally, how to set up smart boundaries so they feel safe and respected.

In step with our online world, widows can even sign up for *virtual* dating coaches, like those of Relationship Hero (relationshiphero .com), a company that has a squadron of internet-based coaches available around the clock. Women who pay for the service will never meet these coaches in person, but they can connect with them virtually—by video, e-chat, or text messages—for help and advice anytime, day or night.

For a professional matchmaker, meanwhile, a widow can expect to pay anywhere from $1,500 and up, with the $5,000 range being the average, depending on how many matches and dates are guaranteed. Some matchmakers are hands-on, handling everything. Others are more hybrid, combining personal matching services with online dating. Most professional matchmakers offer an added safety advantage: They do a background check on the people they represent. Of course, any widow thinking about this option needs to check the bona fides of the companies they are considering, but some people say they have worked.

ANATOMY OF A MATCHMAKING

People who hire matchmakers take the approach that they are investing in happiness. If money truly is no object, there are a handful of elite matchmaking services in the United States that promise discretion and results. Chicago-based Selective Search, founded by Barbie Adler, has a team of twenty matchmakers whose clients include high-profile entrepreneurs, business leaders, and celebrities. The service claims to have an 87 percent success rate in locating the perfect partner.

Matchmaking services are dismissive of online dating. "These apps are filled with fake profiles. Women can get into serious danger. Men are not saying who they really are. So women hire us for vetting," said Lisa Hutcherson, Selective Search vice president of client relations. "With our service, you are not going to be wasting your time."

In their relationship with clients, Hutcherson said the matchmakers are "their advocate, their search agent, their therapist." After a long information-gathering conversation with the matchmaker, often via a video call, Selective Search drafts a program for a potential client. If a woman signs a contract with the company, a matchmaker goes to work combing through an extensive pool of potential matches, sometimes undertaking a nationwide search to find the right match. "Eligible, high-caliber men in their fifties and sixties are hard to find," Hutcherson said.

What does all this personal attention cost? It starts at $50,000 and can ramp up to six figures. A man may pay up to $200,000 to find a woman who checks all his boxes.

Tina, in Connecticut, used Selective Search when her husband died after a thirty-two-year marriage. She lives in a rural town where "everyone is married" and felt her chances of meeting someone on her own were slim.

"I found the Selective Search team members to always be responsive with great follow through. Selective Search also welcomes women as clients. Not all firms do," Tina said. "At my age and station in life, I wanted to be the client, I wanted to be in a position of making a selection. The idea of being in a database waiting for men to choose me was not at all appealing."

When she spoke with us, Tina hadn't yet found a new partner but all the men she was introduced to were "kind, interesting, thoughtful, and successful." She said the company is meeting her goal, which is "to meet men who were similar to me in education, professional success, and who were seeking a new life partner."

Increasingly, however, people of all ages consider the internet the easiest doorway to dating. Several dating apps, including Match.com and eharmony, have blogs, dating tips, webinars, and other services to help subscribers navigate the relationship waters. Widows may also stumble across dating advice and assistance in unexpected places. Public libraries in Connecticut, Illinois, and Montana, for example, launched workshops to teach people how to write profiles for online dating sites.[5] Some churches, too, offer dating seminars and retreats. There are also many independent how-to web essays and blogs to help mid-life daters.

Meeting someone and starting a relationship can happen at any time. People can and do connect face-to-face in serendipitous encounters. (Yes, singles can still meet interesting people in bars.) One of the widows we interviewed found love among the stacks in her local library. Another—a vivacious woman in her early eighties—has never tried a dating app, yet she has gone out on many, many dates and even entered two multiyear relationships. She has met men while working, in the senior-living complex where she has an apartment, and through introductions by friends.

In honing their strategy for finding new romance, some widows who are out dating said it's most effective to have a Plan A—maybe it's online dating—with backup Plan B and Plan C. If a widow is going to dip her toes into online dating, her Plan B might be to connect with a hiking group, join the local historical society, or take an art class. Plan C might be to ask friends to make introductions to single people they know. And, like an investment portfolio, if Plans A, B, or C don't produce the results hoped for, a widow can rebalance her strategy by trying yet another approach.

KNOW THE DEAL BUSTERS

Sometimes loneliness gets in the way of clear-headed thinking. A widow needs to be kind to herself while in the dating scene. She also needs to be honest—to herself and to the people she meets. A widow looking just for fun and companionship should say that. If she wants a dance partner and nothing more, she should be clear about it. Romance can be fun, even without marriage on the horizon.

Lining up potential dates is the first hurdle. Vetting them (while simultaneously undergoing their scrutiny) is the more complicated step. Right off the bat, widows need to identify their nonnegotiables. Smokers? Tattoos? Pets? Porn? Do they require that a potential new partner be financially solvent? Some guidelines will be easy to set, but it is nearly impossible to imagine all the challenges a widow can face when dating. There are—literally—*millions* of website hits dedicated to awful first dates, let alone what follows. Think of the adult man with Ninja Turtle sheets, the suitor who corrected everything that was said, and that guy who went to bed at 9 p.m. (so any movie nights would have to begin at 4 p.m.). We're not making this stuff up.

Barbé and her husband had been a couple for fifteen years before his death from cancer following a misdiagnosis. When she began dating again, she found well-meaning men trying too hard to gain her attention and affection. "I met one fellow who was so keen to go out with me," she said. "I had mentioned that I loved roses and he told me he was a rose grower, so I showed interest. He invited me to his house, a first meeting to look at his roses, and he had picked hundreds of rose petals and paved the entrance to the house with them. It was sweet but, no, not even all those rose petals was going to make him attractive to me.

"It is unbelievable what kinds of things guys come up with," she said.

Margaret, a young widow, had the opposite experience: men who didn't try at all to please. Among her first dates were two where she ended up paying the tab for herself and her date. She said both men had professional jobs—one was a lawyer—and both knew that her husband's death had thrown her into a financial crisis. Yet neither made a move when the check arrived and sat on the table for some time.

Friends are good resources for helping widows come up with their "do" and "don't" lists. As they think through what they want, widows need to remember that perfection probably isn't out there. Indeed, that's what makes humans interesting. The woman who wanted a man who eschewed TV and never wore a baseball cap is still looking. And widows should never try to replicate their previous relationships. That's neither healthy nor productive. The search for new romance is an opportunity to expand life experiences. Widows don't have to love again in the same way they did before.

Many widows spend a lot of time imagining what they'll find in a new partner. A little introspection is also in order. For example, widows should think about whether they might be engineering their deal busters. For people dating widows, the most problematic obstacles include nightstands crowded with photos of the dearly departed spouse or closets full of the deceased partner's clothing, even *years* after they died. There was the woman who compared her boyfriend (often unfavorably) to her husband. Or the widower who, while traveling overseas with his new squeeze, pointed out every place he and his wife had visited in the same country. What about the widow who permanently kept her husband's voice on her answering machine?

For the bereaved, these are loving demonstrations of devotion. For the people dating them, they can be, well, icky.

Even with those who earnestly try to move forward, the ghostly specter of the former spouse can hover in the background. That's because the relationship with the deceased partner continues. The question is whether that old relationship is interfering with the new one. "You know what they say," said a widower who was dating, even though his wife remained in his thoughts, "somebody who marries a widower or widow is marrying a bigamist."

A relationship with a widow requires a healthy ego. Psychologists say being measured against an idealized first husband or wife can spark peculiar jealousy of the deceased partner. They even have a name for it. They refer to it as the Rebecca Syndrome, in a nod to Daphne du Maurier's novel about a woman married to a widower.

A woman told us that widowhood dating, for her, required stepping stones of separation from a deceased spouse. "I remember once when I hosted a dinner party, just after I'd met the man I'm seeing now. I was putting dishes away and I looked up at a photo of my husband and burst into tears. 'I'm pulling away from you. I'm pulling toward someone else,' I was thinking. 'I love you but I'm moving on, baby.' It was hard."

Just as it is difficult for widows to juggle the mixing bowl of emotions that face them, the people they date may find themselves floundering. There will be tone-deaf potential mates who claim a widow "should get over it," failing in a harsh way to understand what bereavement entails. Or people who embrace rigidity when compassion would work better. Or people who weigh in about a widow's children. (Rule No. 1 for Dating Widows: Opinions about offspring—no matter how old they are—are forbidden.)

The fact that serendipitous encounters, online dating, or matchmaking by friends can bring happy results doesn't make them any less nerve-racking. The searching-for-romance landscape can sweep widows back to their younger days when going out with someone new made them jittery and jumpy. Indeed, when reentering the dating scene, a widow might arrive armed with the same dating finesse she had the last time she was out in the world "looking." Widows need to remind themselves that they are taking a big and brave step.

FROM MARTI'S BLOG

Amen. What's Your Email?

I met a guy at Mass. Yes, a Catholic Mass with all its refrains, kneeling, peaceful hand shaking, and singing. I hadn't been going to church much this year, but one Sunday morning in the fall, I decided to check out what is called a Mass Mob (detroitmassmob.com).

Simply explained, this is a trend in some cities (it originated in Buffalo) in which an historic Catholic church in an urban neighborhood hosts a mass for anyone who wants to show up. The Mass Mob typically is promoted in the media but also is on its website. An inner-city church that normally draws seventy-five parishioners on a regular Sunday might see a "mob" of two thousand or more visitors turn up. These events are one-day cash cows for majestic, old churches that are still operating but struggling financially.

When I arrived at 11 a.m., starting time, the pews were filled and only a few folding chairs in the back were still empty. I plunked myself down next to a guy who said he didn't think the person who had been sitting beside him was coming back.

The church was beautiful. A few times during the well-executed Mass, I exchanged words with my seat mate about the marble altar. I'd read that it had been shipped to the church on a barge in the mid-1800s. This church dripped with craftsmanship.

After Mass (I love saying this), Joe (not his real name) and I decided to take an architectural tour of the church, and that led to coffee and conversation in the church hall. After most Mass-goers had cleared out, Joe offered to walk me to my car. But we found ourselves walking around downtown—the conversation continued for a couple more hours—until we ended up at an ice-cream shop. It was as if we were following a 1950s courtship manual, but we just went with it, meeting at church and strolling on a perfect Midwest fall day.

As I got into my car, Joe asked for my work email. I guess he didn't want to be too bold by asking for my phone number. I went to Mass with absolutely no intention of meeting anyone and look what happened.

The next day, he sent me a very nice email at work. We followed it up with a few long phone conversations. It took about two weeks for us to go out. He lives forty miles from me and has a demanding job, he said. My schedule was busy too. But, finally, on a Sunday afternoon, we met for a movie, walked around town, and had dinner. We mused over the meeting at Mass, chuckling, not even sure we had that much in common.

We learned more about each other. I found out he goes to church about twice a month; he discovered I don't. I learned he doesn't drink; he found out I do. He told me he's been single for thirty years. I told him about being married for twenty-eight years and being a widow for almost four years.

The longer we talked, I found out a woman he was supposed to marry bailed just before the wedding day. No explanation. We said our goodbyes as he drove me to my car, and he had one more comment as I slipped out of his car: "Well, you're no shrinking violet." I asked him what that meant. He told me to think about it, but I sort of already knew. This guy thought I was too independent, too outspoken. What a jerk. I never talked to him again. So much for the church meeting.

E-Love

They aren't looking for a pen pal, and if need be, say that.

—Keith Grafman, from *The Art of Instant Message:*
Be Yourself, Be Confident, Be Successful
Communicating Personality

There is nostalgia around traditional dating, a sense that it is a more natural and human way to make connections. Yet, fewer and fewer people rely exclusively on friends' recommendations, workplace meetings, or serendipitous encounters with people in bars or at dinner parties. For better or for worse, online dating is the new normal, with romance seekers routed through posted profiles, texts, emails, and other social media tools.

In many ways, online dating is simply more efficient. The dating pool is larger—tens of millions of people in the United States use online dating websites—and it has been shown to work. Tech tools and artificial intelligence help connect people by location, by interests, and by beliefs more expediently than in-person introductions. Nonetheless, a lot of widows have a love-hate relationship with online romance.

"Rather than looking at it as a torture and dreaded process, commit to doing it for six months and try to approach it with a sense of humor and lightness. Be playful about it," advised Isabella, a widow who dated several men via online apps, including a man fifteen years her junior with whom she was involved for several months. "It can take a long time so be patient. Keep trying. I know two people who have found incredible love online."

Match.com and eharmony are among the best-known apps for meeting singles, but there are many others, including widowsor widowers.com. OurTime.com is a website focused on those over fifty. EliteSingles.com is designed for college-educated people who want to be with other college-educated people. PlentyofFish at POF.com is free. Hinge.co (owned by Match.com) is for people seeking permanent relationships, not hookups, while Herway.com and bumble.com let women initiate the contact. The users of the dating app Ship do the choosing for their friends seeking romance.

There are also websites focused on specific demographics, like religion, culture, or sexual tastes, although the pool of people on them is not as vast as that of Match.com or eharmony. Examples include JDate (Jewish partners), CatholicMatch.com and Christianmingle.com, as well as BlackPeopleMeet.com, AsianDating.com, and LatinAmericanCupid .com. There are gay dating websites, sites for people with disabilities to find partners, and sites for tall people seeking other tall people. Cougar Life.com is for women interested in younger men. Naturistpassion.com is for nudists, while the GlutenfreeSingles page on Facebook is for, obviously, gluten-free daters. Farmersonly.com draws a rural-urban line in the sand. "City folks just don't get it" is its slogan.

When Bobby Goldman, who wrote the musical *Curvy Women*, found herself a widow at barely fifty, her doctors told her to fight her grief by having sex. She spent some unproductive time on Match.com, then signed up for Ashley Madison, the website for people seeking extramarital relationships. Protective of her independence and uninterested in remarrying, she became a serial dater of successful, well-heeled married men.[1] Yes, there's something for everyone.

THE DATING APP EXPERIENCE

The sheer quantity of dating sites to choose from can be dizzying. Before a widow commits to a dating app that charges a fee, she would be wise to sign up for a free limited trial and do some exploring. That way, she can see if she is comfortable with the app's format and the type of responses it draws. It's even routine for people to mix and match, subscribing to more than one dating website at the same time. Whether they embrace this approach may hinge on how much money they want to spend on sites that charge a monthly fee or how much day-to-day time they want to invest in cultivating romance.

Margaret, a young widow, told us that she used her first traditional date after her husband's death as an opportunity to grill the man across the table about the ins and outs of dating apps. "This guy drove quite a distance to see me, and I told him I had never really dated anyone since my husband died," Margaret said. "He was so funny. He said he would tell me everything I needed to know about online dating. One of the things he said is that on the third date you'll probably be sleeping with one another."

When Trudy started dating as a widow, she met several men through friends' introductions, but it was online dating that brought her success. After about a year of dating, her current boyfriend, Justin, moved in, and they are happily living together. A coauthor of this book met a long-term partner via an online site. Many others report that an online meeting led to love.

There is also a large dose of absurdity that arises when artificial intelligence serves as a matchmaker, which is what dating apps are all about. In the *New York Times*' "Tiny Love Stories" feature, a widower wrote that two days after his husband of thirty-one years died, he received an ad from a dating service. (Coincidence? Algorithms at work?) The subject line was "Are they ready for love again?" He laughed at the idiocy. Was forty-eight hours the benchmark for moving on?[2]

For most widows, online dating comes with a learning curve. For starters, they may see fast results in terms of people who show interest, but that doesn't mean they're going to end up in a relationship quickly. It's important to remember that online dating is not a flaw-free tool. Lots of people find love online. Lots. But some people post misleading profiles or try to curry relationships as part of a scam. Widows interested in dating need to trust their instincts. If something feels off-kilter, they should steer clear, regroup, and try a new approach.

"A year after my husband died, I posted a profile online. I have a lot of energy and I look younger than I am—I was sixty-four at the time—so I indicated I was interested in men from forty-nine up," said Monica. "What I found uncanny was that I got a lot of responses from people younger than that. They were strange profiles, a young man who might have a Burmese python hanging around his neck. I don't know what in my profile might have made him think that was acceptable to me.

"After a month, I shut it all down. It felt like a joke." When Monica returned to online dating a year later, using a different site and a new profile, she began to feel more optimistic and less put off by mismatches.

Another widow told us that she discovered the "buff guy" she had been messaging online was using a phony photo and profile. "One day he asked me for $15,000, and I knew it must be a scam," she recalled. "COVID-19 had started so we couldn't get together in person for me to see if he really looked like the photo he was using. But then I saw the same photo in a different profile with a different name." She shut down her dating app account, "let that one roll off my back," and eventually signed up for a different e-dating site.

Marilyn Mendoza, clinical psychiatry instructor at Tulane University Medical Center, warned that if an online prospect seems too good to be true, he or she probably is. "Don't give out too much information. Be careful with what you disclose about yourself," said Mendoza, a bereavement specialist and the author of *We Do Not Die Alone*. Meet in public for coffee or take a walk in an open, busy park, she advised.

Cybercrime, including social media and dating scams, is a colossal problem in the United States (and around the world). The Federal Trade Commission (FTC) reported that money losses from romance scams hit $304 million in 2020, up 50 percent from the previous year. The problem is so insidious that the FTC website has a whole page detailing how the hoaxes are set up and how to report them. Romance and confidence schemes are hard to prosecute, even if money fraud is involved, because people usually turn the money over willingly (then realize they've been scammed).

The hardest hit targets are people aged seventy and over. Widows are earmarked because it is believed their emotional vulnerability can make them trusting. Online watchers say women can test that by signing up for a dating app and then changing their status to "widow." Droves of interested men suddenly appear.

That doesn't mean widows shouldn't use dating apps. They simply need to be on their guard, just as they are with fraudulent emails made to look like they are from legitimate companies (phishing), malicious software (malware) used to plant viruses in computers, and online credit breaches. In fact, online shopping—not internet dating—is the biggest platform for fraud, according to government agencies that monitor cybercrime.

What are the red flags? Widows should run the other way if a person they've connected with online starts asking for money, even small amounts. Sometimes these con men (and women) work with accomplices who back up their phony sob stories. Other warning signs: when an online connection wants to quickly move the conversation off the dating app and onto a private email, messaging, or phone line; when the person showing interest always seems to have a reason why they can't meet in person; or when the potential date is always having emergencies.

Often scammers use photos of other people in their profile. An easy way to check this is to copy the photo and run it through Google Images or TinEye, both websites that identify other places the same photo appears online.

THINGS TO KNOW ABOUT ONLINE DATING

- Widows should be sure to protect their privacy. Online dating sites are intentionally designed to keep personal contact information from being exposed to strangers. Private email addresses or home addresses should not be shared until a widow is sure she is in safe hands. Some people set up a Google phone number and then have those Google calls forwarded to their mobile number so even their phone number remains confidential. Every woman needs to think about security and find her comfort zone.

- Widows should use online photos that they post *only* to dating sites. If they use the same photos on Facebook or LinkedIn or other public sites, it's easier to trace and connect to other personal information that a woman might want to keep confidential for any number of reasons.

- Women considering a dating app should spend a little time checking out the reputation of the website. Big ones, like Match .com or eharmony, have been around a long time and have huge followings, meaning their business sense has been tested. But no-name sites or new startups, well, not so much. The same corporate group that runs Match also owns Hinge.co, French site Meetic, OK Cupid, OurTime, PlentyofFish, Ship, and Tinder. (Hinge.co saw a huge jump in its users when then-presidential contender Pete Buttigieg revealed that is where he met his husband.) Most of these sites charge a monthly fee. No one should turn over their credit card number to a company they're unsure about. It has nothing to do with dating, it's just good consumer behavior.

- It's always a good idea to schedule a first date as a video chat or in a public place, not at home. A coffee shop, the patio at a restaurant, a museum, or a park provide safe meeting grounds. Another smart move is for an e-dater to let her friends know where her date will be. She should arrive in her own transportation and have her cell phone.
- If adult beverages become part of a first date, prudence rules.

THE PROFILE

Getting started online can feel hard. The first step a widow must take is to write a personal description or profile. That can be a big undertaking because widowhood changes people. That forces the "new" person who has emerged from bereavement to craft a description that may not resemble the needs and likes and requirements that once defined her life.

It's important to remember that the online dating profile isn't a test nor is it set in concrete. A widow can keep tweaking her profile and updating her photo, all with the click of a computer keyboard. E-dating coaches say one of the biggest mistakes people make is to *not* update their original profile. Reportedly three-quarters of all online date seekers post a profile and leave it at that. If they're not getting the results they want, refreshing their information should be their first step.

"I spent a lot of time on it," said a widower whose wife died after more than thirty years of marriage. "It made me nervous . . . trying not to sound like I was self-aggrandizing but trying to be straightforward. I'd read about people who put in things that were too personal, or too self-conscious, or even people who had written lies.

"After you've been married so many years, you think of yourself as half of a couple, complementing each other. It was hard to split myself out as an independent person," said the man, who last dated in college. "Also, I didn't know if online dating would be a good option. But I thought it was worth trying."

He briefly tried eharmony then moved to Match.com where, after several months, he found a woman who became his partner for more than ten years. When their relationship ended, he returned to online dating.

Writing an online dating profile also requires some deep thinking about what is wanted in a new partner. In some ways, the use of dating apps seems weirdly like online shopping, except that a widow using a dating app can feel like both the shopper and the shopped. Choosing and posting a profile photo can be nerve-wracking. And there's even a whole new vocabulary that comes with online dating. Ghosting. Catfishing. Cyberstalking. Many websites carry the laundry list of e-dating terms. Here are a few of the best known.

Benching: They like someone, but not enough to make them their exclusive squeeze. They call them, then put them on the back burner for stretches of time. That's benching. As in being on a sports team but never getting to play.

Catfishing: This one doesn't end well. It's when someone lies about their identity or background online. (It's not illegal to use a false identity online, except when a line is crossed into fraud.) People who catfish may build the phony profile to bilk others out of money or valuables. Or maybe they're just living out a fantasy. Usually, there will be a lot of online activity, but the widow may never get to meet the person on the other end of her message traffic.

Don't confuse catfishing with hatfishing. That's when a man wears a hat in his online photo to disguise that he's bald or balding.

Cyberstalking: This is the repeated use of electronic communications to harass or scare someone. Over-the-internet harassment can take many forms, from threatening emails to the use of cell phones or social media to keep track of someone's whereabouts. Cyberstalking is like regular stalking, an alert that the person is an abuser.

Dickpic: This is when a man sends a photograph of his penis, usually unsolicited. For some reason, men think people want to see their nether regions.

Friends with benefits: Friends, sex, no commitment. (The other, cruder, name for this is f*ckbuddies.)

Ghosting: Let's say a widow has established an online relationship with someone. The two exchange email or text messages regularly. Then suddenly the person at the other end of this budding virtual relationship disappears without a word. The widow has been ghosted. This is hurtful and is usually accompanied by, at first, great worries about the other person and, then, great anger.

LDR: This is shorthand for long-distance relationship, meaning that the potential daters are willing to extend the geographic radius for how far they'll travel for romance.

LTR: This is short for long-term relationship, as in someone's online profile describing them as "Looking for an LTR."

One widow told us she had a playful, yet intense, back-and-forth with a man on a dating app for some time before finally meeting. "We met, had a great day together, and then he ghosted me—I didn't even know what that word meant at the time," she said. "It made me furious but after some months, I contacted him again, and we were back in touch. We went to a music festival and started seeing each other more often, but then he would—again—let long stretches go by without getting in touch.

"He said it was just his way, that he was a recluse and at times just has to disappear, but I realized that also meant I couldn't depend on him for any kind of long-term, caring, loving relationship."

Most people ask themselves two critical questions when they are preparing their online profiles: What will I reveal about myself? What am I looking for in a new partner? There's one golden rule: less is more. Still, even brief profile descriptions can be specific—and that's what makes them stand out. Rather than writing "I like wine outdoors after work," a more specific profile might say "a glass of pinot grigio in an Adirondack chair on a lazy afternoon is my happy time." A widow's profile should offer a peek into who she is.

When it comes to a new romantic interest, many online daters make the mistake of laundry-listing what they want in a partner ("they must be tall, employed, and as comfortable loading the dishwasher as fixing the car") rather than sharing what they will bring to a relationship. A widow needs to steer clear of making her preferences sound like those job ads that seek someone who speaks three languages and multitasks in every skill area. If there is something that *must* be in a relationship, sure, that should be made clear. But a widow should never assume that, for all its efficiencies, that online dating is the opportunity to find perfection. Indeed, most people find that it is healthiest to ditch the notion of a perfect mate and, instead—or even more importantly—imagine what kind of life they want to live.

There are plenty of resources available to help widows take these baby steps back into the dating world. For starters, they can call their besties. This is what friends are for. Best friends can help online dating candidates realize their strengths and attributes—as well as point out the things that rock their world. Friends know them better than anyone. They can even help take the profile photo that lets a widow's personality shine.

When it comes to photos, a Google search will turn up tips on the best online dating photos. Some of the advice is easy. Don't take a photo with weird angles that distort the face. Don't wear sunglasses and a hat that makes the person's face impossible to see. Don't use photos that are years old or post an image amid a group of people. One good rule of thumb is to use a photo that shows what a widow probably will look like on a first date.

Writer Emily Ladau wrote an interesting piece for the *New York Times* on her fear that men would bypass her online profile because she uses a wheelchair. Ladau, a disability rights activist, wrote that dates with her can sometimes feel like crash courses on disability, and that's not easy for some people. At first, she hid her disability. Her wheelchair wasn't visible in her profile photo, and she waited to make a connection before she told the rest of her story. But then she decided to be upfront about something that is core to her identity. She made it part of her profile and that made a difference—to her and to the people she dated online.[3]

Rather than making the photo process feel like homework (or worse), the least stressful approach is to try to make it fun. A woman can tuck a favorite book, evidence of a hobby, or something significant to her in her photo—and then wait to see if anyone responding to her profile has noticed.

In many ways, the hardest part of online dating for widows is also the hardest part of any kind of dating, and that is rejection. A widow has already been left by someone she loved. Why expose her fragile self to the judgment of strangers? Neuroscientists have found that the physiological reaction to being dumped or being left out is the same physiological response that comes from physical pain. In effect, humans are wired to process rejection as something worse than it is. Evolutionary scientists say such overreaction harkens back to tribal times when rejection meant someone was booted out by their clan and left to fend for themself in an unwelcoming and unsafe world. Today, the repercussions of rejection are far less severe. The best approach? Don't take it personally.

In the case of online dating, that means not over-worrying about being passed over by a stranger. Most of the time, it's not about the widow or her profile. Many factors are at play when people scrutinize e-dating sites. Widows who can be nonchalant about *not* being liked, winked at, swiped, given a thumbs-up, whatever else the site uses to indicate interest will have an easier time of it. Most online daters feel daunted by the first rejections but, once they're at it long enough, they realize that it's not them, it's the circumstances.[4]

The challenge of online dating is the "keeping at it" bit. Some experienced online daters suggest trying at least three dates with the same person if there's any interest at all before moving to the next person. Others suggest dating at least three people at the same time which, if nothing else, ensures a busy social life. It's OK to take a break from dating apps when they become overwhelming or discouraging. Before doing so, a widow might give herself a small goal. It could be to go out on two—or even just one—more dates before tossing in the towel. Maybe she should refresh her profile and give it another week online. Or perhaps she should invest some time in listening to a dating podcast for midlife romance seekers to see if it gives her any new ideas.

And what should a widow do if she meets someone who isn't quite right? Be kind. Constructive criticism, after all, is still criticism. She should practice the simple words, "I don't think you are a match for me."

It can take time to meet the right person. This isn't a sprint. It is usually not useful to set timetables or deadlines, which can end up being sources of frustration. If possible, a widow should try to approach online dating as a new, possibly entertaining, adventure. Widows need to keep their sense of humor when dating.

If a first date doesn't lead to a second date, there is no need to despair. A bad date can be a learning opportunity. Certainly, it can be fodder for a good laugh with friends. If a date was pleasant but didn't lead to a romance, it can be valued for the fact it took a widow out dancing or to a movie or into a conversation that made her think about something in a different way. If it is an especially happy date but no sparks fly, the widow might not have met a new romantic partner but maybe she's on the path to a new friendship.

FROM MARTI'S BLOG

Widows' Choice: Divorced, Never Married or Widowed?

By now, some might say I'm giving a little too much thought to this online dating stuff. I don't want this to turn into a blog on cyber dating; I think there is enough of those already. But at this stage of widowhood, I can't help but explore it—mostly because it is there, and where the hell else do you meet men at my age?

As is my nature, I'm investigating it—almost as an outsider. It is highly controllable and follows a routine. Maybe a guy emails a few times. He sends his phone number, and it is up to me to call. A telephone conversation reveals whether there is any connection, and it may or may not lead to a meeting. A meeting tells you both if you want it to go further.

One of my widow friends is in the same place. She had a five-and-a-half-year relationship that recently went south, which led her to the online world.

We talk about our experiences. We laugh and reassure each other that this is not easy and takes a surprising amount of energy. We compare notes; we wax on about our good-guy husbands and how our former lives were so much better, richer, full of love and comfort.

We regret that the majority of these online prospects are divorced. Then we pose the question: Which is the greater evil? Divorced—once, twice, or three times, widowed, or never married? It is amusing fodder for our frivolous conversations. I seem to have run into twice-divorced more than I like. I try to be open-minded, but I carry ingrained biases. We widows can be judgmental, thinking we are somehow better than the people who have botched marriages. We are not always nice.

I've gone out with a couple of widowers who, unfortunately, seem to have their own set of issues. However, even if there is zero chemistry, you feel more of a connection with a widower purely because you've been in a similar boat and can commiserate.

Finally, there's the baffling world of the never marrieds. I've had a spate of interest from never marrieds. For some reason, I think online daters who have never married gravitate toward widows, though I have no research to substantiate this. Frankly, if you had a long, fruitful marriage and raised kids, it is tough to relate to someone who has experienced neither.

Even though I have limited time talking to never marrieds, I think I'm done with that demographic. And the multiple-divorced guys recently have fallen a few notches on my ladder; they seem to hate the institution of marriage.

I know I shouldn't make such pronouncements because you just never know what is going to work, and life just keeps surprising me.

• 5 •

Don't Stand So Close to Me

The very least you can do in your life is figure out what you hope for. And the most you can do is live inside that hope. Not admire it from a distance but live right in it, under its roof.

—Author Barbara Kingsolver, in *Animal Dreams*

The Irish mini-documentary, *How to Fall in Love in a Pandemic*, records the fledgling relationship of two film directors who met just before the world went on novel coronavirus lockdown. The protagonists, Mimi and Michael-David, connected on Tinder and spent a weekend together in Chicago before Michael-David returned to his home in Ireland. They had such a good time together that Mimi flew to Dublin two weeks later, envisioning five days with her new love interest.

Then suddenly, the COVID-19 pandemic became the headline. Mimi's flight home was canceled, and Ireland was ordered into lockdown. Mimi and Michael-David were trapped together . . . indefinitely.

COVID-19 upended innumerable aspects of life around the world, romance included. Quick-acting, rule-obeying countries provided hope that quarantine restrictions would not disrupt dating forever. As the months went by, tests became more accessible, faster, and more trustworthy. Contact tracing was used by greater numbers of public health departments across the United States. Then vaccinations—the "Get Out of Jail Free" card for daters—appeared. Even as new customs and protocols were getting anchored more soundly, it felt inevitable that one day the usual rules of romance, or at least a more recognizable version of them, would return.

Then why do we have a chapter on pandemic dating?

We already know mask-wearing and other COVID-19-related protocols might weave in and out of our lives for a long time yet. Some scientists have even warned that coronavirus outbreaks (and mutations of the virus) could arrive in waves every winter from now on. If true, the ability to reimagine the rules of dating or, at least, to understand the threshold for risk, may be essential for romance in the future. The arrival of the pandemic also made many daters think even more about their health; some are adopting healthier living goals that are spilling over into their dating preferences. At the same time, the aloneness of the pandemic pushed some widows to ramp up their commitment to seeking a new relationship. Despite the risk, this was their nudge to get back into dating.

"COVID had me thinking that I'd like to meet someone I can pod-up with. The isolation of the lockdowns and the quarantines has really brought that realization home to me," said one widow.

CLOCK-WATCHING

For many people, especially older daters, the pandemic boosted their sense of urgency about finding a new partner. Would the romance time-line speed up as a hedge against the next lockdown? Would the crisis reveal strength, even heroism, that would fast-forward what otherwise must be more hard-won courtships?

Margaret met a man in January 2020 and by March 15, when pandemic restrictions were in the works, she invited him to move in with her. "The thing about being a young widow is that I was willing to step over everything because I was so desperate to be loved again. With this man, I thought that I had hit the jackpot. He was such a charmer," she said. After the new beau and his two children moved into the home she shared with her three teenagers, she realized it was a colossal mistake—and challenging to get him to leave.

"It was a disaster. It was a dysfunctional relationship," Margaret said. "My children and friends still love me, but that's the only good thing that came out of it."

Scott, meanwhile, found that COVID-19 made it hard to move forward on a promising new relationship with Nina, a widow he met online. Scott, a widower, had ended a long-term relationship just weeks before the pandemic lockdown was announced, and his post-breakup loneliness was made even more acute by his inability to see friends regularly. Once he felt ready to date again, some of the initial COVID-19 restrictions had been loosened, but the danger was still there, particularly for a seventy-one-year-old man.

Like Scott, Nina felt isolated. After many online and phone chats, they decided they were willing to try an in-person date. "She was even more cautious about it than me," Scott said. "We talked about how well we had been obeying the public health precautions. We talked about masks and social distancing. We decided to meet for a drink at an outdoor patio."

Some romance seekers asked potential mates to get a COVID-19 test just before any in-person commitments, but Scott and Nina did not feel that was necessary. One in-person date turned into a couple more, always at outdoor venues, until Scott and Nina decided to risk a quick kiss. "It was nice but it is hard to keep the energy going when you can't see one another on a regular basis," Scott said. "I really want and need more in a relationship."

Although the COVID-19 quarantine immediately altered the dating landscape, the enigma of the human experience was evident. Where one might think that people would hunker down and swear off dating until the coast was clear, the pandemic instead sparked a huge uptick in the number of people online looking for love connections. Messaging on the dating app Hinge.co skyrocketed. The Bumble app had nearly a million users adopt a "virtual dating badge" on their profile, a sign that they wanted to continue dating via video and phone calls. Two months after lockdowns started rolling across the United States, Bumble issued a statement indicating that video calls among its members were up nearly 70 percent from the levels posted before the pandemic.

Other dating apps without video-calling options added them. Many online daters continued relying on video calls even after it was safe again to meet in person. Before vaccines were available, dating apps saw users mentioning their COVID-19 test results in their profiles. Once vaccinations started, the use of the terms "vaccine" and "antibodies" rose, and some people added "vaccinated" to their online status. Others made clear they had no intention of getting the shots. The dating site OKCupid reworded its compatibility questionnaire to include "Will you

get the COVID-19 vaccine?" People who were vaccinated reported seeing ramped up interest from other online daters.

DATING DISRUPTED

The pandemic forced a reimagining of the rules of dating or, at least, a
reckoning with the threshold for risk that people will accept—or disregard, in many cases—as they seek romance. A survey in April 2020,
when the pandemic lockdown was at its first peak in most states, found
that nearly one-in-four young Americans broke quarantine to have sex.
The survey by Everlywell, which makes at-home medical tests, including for COVID-19, focused on a representative sample of US adults ages
twenty to thirty-one, so it's not possible to say how frequently older
adults—or widows, specifically—were taking chances.[1] However, some
widows we interviewed told us they had sex with partners who did not
live with them during the pandemic.

There was, of course, no indication that COVID-19 was sexually
transmitted through semen or vaginal fluids, but physical proximity—an
integral part of sex—was the bigger danger. Public health officers around
the globe started making suggestions about how to juggle dating amid
disease. Some called for monogamy, signaling an end to serial dating,
while others recommended wearing a mask and avoiding kissing during
sex. The Mayo Clinic website counseled that masturbation was the saf-
est form of sex during the pandemic. For its part, Planned Parenthood
suggested more sexting and even intimate videos between consenting
partners who were physically apart, while New York City's Health
Department tried to make COVID-19 sex sound fun by encouraging
people to "make it a little kinky" and "be creative with sexual positions
and physical barriers, like walls, that allow sexual contact while preventing close face to face contact."[2]

Interestingly, during COVID-19, older widows responded more
responsibly to public health protocols. That's because older people, especially women, are less likely to believe misinformation and disinforma-
tion, including conspiracy theories and false claims about the pandemic.
A fifty-state COVID-19 survey found that people under twenty-five
were the most gullible when it came to fake news about the novel coronavirus. At the same time, women of all ages were more likely to use

personal protection equipment, including face masks, than men. (This is a trend that was spotted in previous pandemics, too.)

One study looked at nearly two thousand five hundred adults in the United States and found that "men more than women agree that wearing a face covering is shameful, not cool, a sign of weakness, and a stigma."[3] Years of research have shown that women are better at hand-washing, too—a key protocol for preventing the spread of contagion—and that remained true during the COVID-19 pandemic. What does this mean for widows interested in finding new romantic partners during public health challenges? They may have to negotiate yet another layer of safety into dating (if they are dating men).

Some pandemic-related public health protocols could be incorporated into our lives long term. Zoom dating, too, may remain as an entrenched part of the romance scene, at least during the early meet-and-greet stages of dating. So how do people meeting online determine if they have chemistry? Marilyn Mendoza, the clinical psychiatry instructor at Tulane, said that because technology like Zoom puts people face-to-face on a screen, it feels a lot like going out to meet but it has an important weakness. "It's a way to connect with someone, but it's hard to create intimacy," she said.

Mendoza is a strong advocate of caution when doing online dating, particularly for older widows who had decades-long marriages. She recommends that widows keep the conversation strictly online until they have a chance to really know someone. Normally a proponent of meeting new romantic partners through the recommendations of friends, family, or coworkers, she acknowledged that was difficult during a pandemic. And therein lies the problem. While the pandemic strengthened the desire to be with someone, it also made the whole process of meeting a partner both more difficult and more dangerous. Health aside, it also upped the romance con game. Romance scams soared during the pandemic.

The novel coronavirus underpinned the dating game with new and greater calculations of risk. Age, health, the local COVID-19 infection rate, and autoimmune illnesses that made people vulnerable to the coronavirus suddenly became factors to weigh. This prompted frank discussions of people's risk aversion, including stepped-up discussions of sex and safety. How far would people go—especially early in a courtship—to make the sacrifices required to become their own "safe pod" or "bubble," agreeing not to take risks so that they could safely interact with one another to the exclusion of others? Post-COVID, those risk considerations and conversations will not necessarily disappear.

Earlier in the pandemic, two basic rules hovered over dating: to-mask or not-to-mask and what constituted social distancing. But humans are quick to adapt to new circumstances and many did in the pursuit of romance. Masks quickly turned into fashion statements. Women traded in medical masks for face coverings that were cute and sometimes sexy. Some men tied scarves around their heads, covering their noses and mouths to create a bohemian look. As for social distancing, how close were people on a date willing to get? Would they agree to a date out-doors? Would there ever be a chance for a kiss? What about virtual sex via FaceTime or Zoom?

Isabella had started a relationship right before the pandemic hit. "Suddenly it was all about taking a test or having a good sense of where each of us had been before we got together. We've only been able to see one another in person about four times," she said. "We met for a long bike trip, but he is being very cautious. We're not having sex.

"I know there's some risk involved, but there's also some risk in living in isolation," she added.

Another widower, early into a relationship, made an even more dramatic decision. Larry, a retired automotive employee, made his first foray into dating just before COVID-19 began its worldwide spread. Larry spotted a woman one day while getting coffee after a church meeting. They said hello. "It was two years since my wife died and I needed to do something with my life," he said. "I had vowed in the new year to be more proactive."

He ran into the same woman a month later when working out in the gym at his city park. She was attending the movie theater at the park with her friends. They chatted a bit and planned to get together. Their first date came less than a month before COVID-19 hit their state, Michigan, hard.

Larry was trying to get used to dating again—after thirty-seven years of marriage to the same woman—and he was doing it during a pandemic. The new couple took the big step of quarantining together. "It is important to be straightforward with each other from the start," Larry said. "You have to be on the same page as to how the relationship will go."

Their story unfolded more happily than that of Isabella. Tucked in together during the pandemic, Larry and his girlfriend were both careful about spending time with others. Larry continued his outdoor activities with friends, such as fishing and bike riding. But as a couple, they generally eschewed socializing with others. Most of their out-of-the-house activities together involved walks—without masks.

Once 2021 rolled around and vaccines became available, the risk calculations changed. Even with vaccinations, some people worried about the new virus variants popping up. And, of course, there was the segment of the population that refused to be vaccinated.

When the coronavirus hit the United States, there was a notion that it would be tamed quickly and things would return to normal by Memorial Day 2020—which, even at that, seemed like a big sacrifice. But as the pandemic stretched toward its year anniversary, the prospect of getting "back to normal" was shuffled further into the future. Scientists talked about how the pandemic wouldn't end with the appearance of the vaccine alone but would continue until the majority of the population is immune, which could mean into 2022. In mid-2021, with more than a third of the US population fully vaccinated, new perspectives emerged, including the idea that the United States would never reach herd immunity. The "new normal" is still taking shape, influenced not only by where the country is heading but also by the lessons learned through the COVID-19 surges and waves of lockdowns.

Some pundits suggested that dating during coronavirus—free from sex and distractions—offered an opportunity to talk and really get to know someone. Others maintained that people are wired for human touch and a contact-free life ran counter to that.

SO MANY NEW WIDOWS

Beyond issues of risk, there is another aspect of the pandemic with special resonance for widows seeking romance. The pandemic and its lockdowns altered the process of bereavement for the newest widows, even if their partners did not die from COVID-19. Grieving became crueler, harsher for women who were barred from saying a private good-bye in a natural way. Researchers are already investigating what they refer to as "pandemic grief" to understand the distinctive ways it has made the anguish of loss more profound and how it has disrupted the way people heal from the death of a partner.

Medical experts have long known that men are more susceptible to viruses in general. COVID-19 was no exception. Women have stronger immune responses to viruses; genetic and hormonal differences may be factors, too. With the novel coronavirus death toll disproportionately affecting men, one of its tragic consequences was the advent of "Coronavirus Widows." Not only were the sheer numbers of deaths from the pandemic staggering, but the public health crisis heaped additional trauma on a new generation of widows forced to live with the hardcore cruelty of a spouse dying a painful death alone. Coronavirus widows met their loss unaccompanied; some were even sick themselves. No hugs were given to many of these widows as their circles of support were kept at bay by new public health rules. Sometimes friends and family were even barred from attending a funeral.

After thirty-seven-year-old Lew Berry died of COVID-19 in northern Indiana, his wife, Brianna Berry, launched a Facebook page she called "COVID-19 Widows and Widowers Support Group" and then watched its membership grow.[4] It was just one of many support groups that surfaced as the death toll rose. Grief naturally isolates widows. The pandemic took that to an extreme.

The pandemic also served as a callback to how fleeting life can be. Perhaps it was not a grief trigger in the usual sense, but the flood of obituaries in the newspapers—day after day as hundreds of thousands of Americans died—reminded many widows of the emotions they, too, lived through when their partners died. In tandem, it made them recall their own mortality and the people they have outlived. For some, it deepened their resolve to forge a new relationship while there is still time.

FROM MARTI'S BLOG

Finding a Companion in the Nick of Time

Another one of my unattached widower friends has joined the world of the attached. He met her at church shortly before COVID-19 hit the world, and everything, at least for now, seems to be going well for these two Catholics.

She has a couple twenty-something children and he has three grown boys. Although there is not much they can do to pass the time together during COVID (or so he says), they keep each other company. The relationship has eased their loneliness, and he is finding comfort with this new partner.

He and I were always just friends starting during the end of his wife's illness. After she died, he reached out to me to further our friendship. With my serious illness, it was clear this would never be more than a casual friendship.

Larry, we will call him, is a good guy although extremely politically conservative. We share values though and raised our children similarly. I liked his wife; I'm not sure how he felt about my husband. His wife died three years ago; my husband has been gone almost nine years. Both our spouses died of different kinds of brain cancer.

He invited me over for a swim in his pool and made me lunch one summer weekday. It was pleasant. He said, "Remember when I told you I would tell you if I started dating someone? Well, I'm dating someone."

He went on to say this relationship would not impact our friendship. Our bond as widow-and-widower—and friends—is important to him. He said to call him soon for a bike ride.

I said I would, but I haven't. I'm not sure our friendship will stay the same. We used to go to lunch and drive around the city looking for new spots to check out. We walked and rode bikes. He spent many hours at my house making repairs. I made him meals of thankfulness.

But now I'm getting sicker. My cancer has leapt from a multitude of bones to small mounds of soft tissue in the liver and lungs. Overall, I don't feel great. I long for how I used to feel. But better days could be on the docket. I am hopeful as a new treatment is about to start. As for Larry with his partner, he is smiling more frequently.

I'm happy for him.

· 6 ·

Sex

Sex is one of the nine reasons for reincarnation. The other eight are unimportant.

—Writer Henry Miller

The remarkable bliss of skin against skin.

For widow Gretchen, sex with a new partner was joyful. "Intimacy was one of the things I really missed," she said. "My late husband and I had not been intimate for the last ten years of his life. I missed lying in bed talking with a partner and other moments like that." Life improved for her when she found a partner eight years younger. She was much older than the last time she was sexually active—but she was not ashamed of her body, a sentiment she attributed to her European upbringing.

The desire for sex is normal. Even when a woman is a widow. Even when a woman is older. Sometimes even when a widow is in the middle of grief. "One of the hardest things about being a widow is being alone in your bed," said Barbé, who was married for fifteen years before her husband died.

In the early days of widowhood, many women feel they will never want sex again. Some hang onto that feeling for a long time, unable to imagine physical contact with anyone but their absent spouse. But others wake up one day longing for the intimacy and the human connection that comes with good sex. Their friends might try to explain it away, telling them that they are simply missing touch and hugs, and maybe a day with the grandchildren or a good massage is all they need. That's part of the mythology stamped onto older women, that they can't or shouldn't feel sexual.

What is really happening is that these widows are experiencing what researchers refer to as "sexual bereavement." Their sex drive has kicked back on, even if their heart still feels broken. Although that feeling may seem in conflict, startling, even a betrayal, it is perfectly normal. A spouse or partner has died, but the widow is still alive, lamenting the loss of sexual expression, which is part of a rich, multidimensional life.

The craving for sex after her husband died helped nudge Gretchen into the dating world. Not so for Susanna, who felt comfortable with her body but had no interest in physical intimacy without an emotional link. She was cautious when she met an interesting man three years into her widowhood journey.

"I didn't dive right in. I had been without intimacy for a significant period of time and I wanted to work up to it, to decide first if I wanted a relationship with this person," Susanna said. "I've always been a prude about getting things started, but once we did, it was good."

For Louise, meanwhile, a new relationship brought levels of passion she hadn't experienced in her marriage. And Margaret, who lost a striking amount of weight in her quest to become healthy after her husband's death, said good sex is a requirement for any new relationship. "I am different than I was when I was in a sexual relationship with my husband. I have a whole new body, and I want to take it out on the town," she explained. "A man in any new relationship for me has to have a good sex drive. I'm not negotiating that."

Another widow said sex was the reason she is interested in younger men, whom she sees as more virile and energetic.

MISSING PHYSICAL CONTACT

The death of a partner means no more cuddling, caressing, or canoodling. No more regular (sometimes rapturous) sex. No more snuggling into an adjacent warm body in the bed each morning or each night. Gone is the sensation of a head resting on a shoulder while watching TV. Absent is the handholding when the plane is landing, the sweet affection that comes with couplehood.

While the primal drive for physical contact can be part of what pushes widows to seek new relationships, getting naked with a new person can be difficult, complicated, and downright scary. Widows may need to do some mental rewiring to jump into bed without any emotional attachment. And friends and family—accustomed to thinking of a left-behind spouse as part of a permanent partnership—can become unnerved when a widow starts talking about dating, let alone having sex again.

It is wrong to let sex sit like the unaddressed elephant in the room. Sex in widowhood can be energizing. It can also be healing.

Widows who begin dating are likely to return to sex as if it were a huge adventure. This may be the first time in twenty, thirty, forty, or more years they've been intimate with someone new. While a widow's first forays in the bedroom may be nerve-racking, or even clumsy, they also may be wonderfully exciting, bringing something between the pheromone coupling of a pair of high schoolers and the joyful pleasure that comes from knowing one's body—and needs—well. Sex with a new partner also offers a chance to experiment, especially if the other person is curious, open-minded, more experienced, or all three.

Trudy, a public relations and marketing specialist, said having sex for the first time after her husband died was not "nearly as awkward as I would have thought." The couple took it slow and "felt comfortable and safe with each other in bed."

"It had been a long time so there was certainly pent-up desire," she said. "There was also a lot of attraction."

Widows considering sex should ask themselves: What are my sexual guidelines? Do I want to share my bedroom history, and do I expect a new partner to talk about his or her past experiences? Do I even understand what being "exclusive" means? Honestly, the exclusive talk can open up a whole new world for someone who has been in a thirty-plus year marriage, long before monogamy-while-dating became a bargaining issue.

Some widows seek out sexual contact even though they have no interest in relationships. In some ways, sex after bereavement—but before new attachment—can serve as a safeguard. While pursuing lusty experiences with no strings attached, a widow may be less likely to confuse sex and love. For widows also seeking an emotional connection, a sexual relationship forces into play a conversation about monogamy.

Is the new partner dating others and having sex with them, too? If the answer is "yes," a widow needs to understand how that makes her feel and, more importantly, how safe sex aware this new adventure will be. Widowhood offers no special protection against HIV-AIDS and the slew of sexually transmitted diseases that someone in a long-term relationship rarely thinks about.

SHARING EXPERIENCES

People range tremendously on what they share. Some offer too much information; others remain extraordinarily closed-mouth.

Andrew hesitated about becoming sexual after his wife died. "I didn't really know how committed I could be to a relationship. I was still trying to figure stuff out, and I didn't see any kind of physical or sexual connections," he said. Months later, when he did feel ready to date again, he avoided telling people he was a thirty-six-year-old widower.

"I was—and still am—hesitant about talking about the death of my wife. I pretty much kept that conversation within my immediate circle," he said. "If I went out on a date, it would be two or three conversations later when it came out." He said he took that road because he "didn't want people to see me as a tragic figure."

"I thought women might see me as carrying something too heavy for them to take on," he explained.

This posture is the opposite of what many women find when they date widowers. Some women we spoke with found that widowed men often made a point of telling them about their loss because they believed it opens the door to a "sympathy fuck."

"I became involved with someone who was always trying to play the sympathy card, wanting me to feel sorry for him because of his tragic loss," Trudy said. "He used this with both friendship and with sex to get the result he wanted."

Doug, a widower, said he inadvertently found himself in that role. Doug's wife suffered through a protracted illness before dying, and he took his time before he dated again. But long before he was ready for commitment, this nearly seventy-year-old widower felt ready for sex. So, he packed an elegant picnic and asked out a woman who had caught his fancy. They spent a delightful afternoon in the fresh air, talking, eating, drinking wine.

Since he'd brought together all the right romantic components, his A-game, so to speak, he was flummoxed when the woman didn't want to go to bed with him. They continued dating and, with time, they became intimate, but he acknowledged that he misjudged his strategy. The woman who turned him down said his "nervous" sexual advances felt aggressive.

Long-time widow Carole Radziwill, author of the novel *The Widow's Guide to Sex and Dating,* has said in interviews that widows, too, can find themselves channeling everything toward sex. She was thirty-six when her husband—the son of Lee Radziwill and nephew of Jacqueline Kennedy Onassis—died of cancer. "You think that because something so profound has happened, you're going to emerge a much deeper person, but sexually all you want to do is get laid," she told the *New York Times* in a 2014 article.[1] "There was a time after Anthony died, a long phase, where I was just wearing see-through clothes . . . and dating younger men."

The return to an active sex life is a reawakening for some widows. Where grief blunted the edges of emotion, intense physical relationships sharpens them again. Sexual curiosity, neither naïve nor vulgar, is one among many healthy steps toward rebuilding a life that has been gutted by death.

Some women interviewed for this book pointed out that since widowhood often happens later in life, there may be additional considerations related to sex and aging, developments that might have been easier to handle in tandem with long-time spouses than with bumbling new partners. For starters, a widow might not be as agile as she once was. Lubrication and condom use typically need to be discussed. Partners may have performance anxiety. One woman described her first time in bed with an overzealous widower: "It was the worst sex ever."

After that initial debacle, however, subsequent encounters went "very well." The motto of that story? It can take time for a widow to find her equilibrium in a new sexual relationship. The plus to this is that widows usually know their bodies, and what satisfies them, better than when they were younger.

Overall health, as well as where a widow falls on the menopause spectrum, also affects new sexual encounters. Health challenges, among them heart issues, diabetes, and cancer, often climb as people get older. Some of these illnesses affect energy levels, strength, and sexual performance. External issues can also affect one's sex life, widowed or not. Depression, alcohol abuse, and sleeplessness can hamper sexual satisfaction. The overuse of smartphones, electronic tablets, and television watching has also been found to dilute intimacy.

For widows, depression is a common problem, although it tends to diminish with time. Studies have found that the prevalence of depression is highest in the first month of widowhood, although it can remain above the level of the general population as long as five years after the death of a spouse or partner. Unfortunately, a common medical response—antidepressants—can lower libido.

Sex can be tricky, too, when it comes to adjusting to new partners and their needs after being accustomed to the same person and familiar rituals and patterns. Sometimes, guilt joins the mix. One widow said she almost felt as if her deceased husband was watching her. "I wanted to say, 'I'm sorry, but I'm tired of being alone.'"

For many of these challenges, there are workarounds. The National Institute on Aging website has an entire page focused on the most common issues affecting sexuality in later life—from arthritis and vaginal dryness to medication side effects and incontinence—with suggestions on how to address them.[2] Important to remember is that regardless of age, there is also a psychological component to the best sex. It's not all about bodies. And good sex goes hand-in-hand with good communication. Widows need to prepare themselves to talk about it—what they want, what they like, what they worry about. Those issues may look very different than they did in marriage.

Monica said erotica and sex that does not necessarily involve penetration now hold more interest for her. "When I sleep with someone again, it would have to be someone who would accept the wide range of what intimacy can be. I would not be opposed to mutual masturbation, for example," she said. "And I would prefer my partner to be someone healthy and virile. I don't want to deal with things like Viagra."

Although the desire to share a bed returns for many widows, even those who vowed they'd never have sex again, it doesn't come back for everyone. Some widows cannot get past the feelings of guilt, the sense that they would be cheating on their (now dead) husbands. Others might have lived in sexless or lackluster marriages and find it too difficult to build new patterns. Some have filled their lives with other, more satisfying, nonsexual connections.

Jennifer was married for forty years to a fit, athletic man, but she said their marriage deteriorated and they had little in common in the years before he died. She now has no interest in sex. "Even though I don't want to be with women sexually, the most interesting and satisfying relationships I have are with women friends," Jennifer said. "I don't even like older men—they're boring—and I have no interest in sexual intimacy with them."

Medical conditions may preclude satisfying sexual contact. A choice of celibacy might be tied to religious beliefs. Some widows may prefer to redirect their sexual energy into other pursuits, or even toward self-love. (Vibrator to the rescue!) Others say quite plainly, "I'm done," when it comes to dating and sex. They had a satisfying marriage and believe that can't be repeated.

Although not common, a widow may even enter a new romance with a partner who is willing to forgo full sexual intimacy. The important thing is for both people to talk honestly about their needs and expectations.

INTERCOURSE, OUTERCOURSE, AND SEXUALLY TRANSMITTED DISEASES

Some older widows find there is something liberating about sex once there is no fear of pregnancy, no children to take care of, no grueling schedule to keep. Age does not, however, provide one important protection. It is no barrier to sexually transmitted diseases (STDs), which are also sometimes known as sexually transmitted infections (STIs).

The older people are, the less resilient their immune systems, making it easier to contract diseases. Physicians frequently neglect to discuss STDs with older patients, and older adults often are ignorant about the risk, especially if they begin dating after years in a monogamous marriage. A long marriage may also be a reason why they are unaccustomed to using condoms, dental dams—the thin latex sheets people use to avoid direct contact during safe oral sex—and other barriers that can help protect against STDs during sex. Many STDs do not have obvious symptoms.

Older adults do not lead the country in STDs—that dubious honor goes to teens and young adults—but the STD rate for people age fifty or older is significant. According to the Centers for Disease Control and Prevention (CDC), older adults accounted for one of every six new HIV diagnoses in the United States in 2018.[3] Other prevalent STDs that widows should know about include chlamydia, gonorrhea, herpes, and, for those hooking up with bisexual men, syphilis. A widow's primary physician, Planned Parenthood, and community health departments provide testing. The CDC website allows individuals to type in their zip code to find testing sites and to help determine what tests might be appropriate.[4]

One awkward issue with STDs is that some widows have no idea how or when to launch that conversation. These are subjects that weren't on the table the last time most widows dated. When we asked women about cautions they took or conversations they had before sex in widowhood, their responses ranged from "Whoops. I guess I should have thought about that" to "I just trusted that my partner was safe."

A young widow acknowledged she knew about the risks of STDs because she had discussed them with her teenage children. However, she took no precautions herself the first time she went to bed with a new partner. "I trusted that he hadn't been with anybody for a couple of years. That was stupid. There's no way I should have done that," she said. "But I trust men. I trusted my husband.

"There's a learning curve I'm struggling with here," she added. "For example, condoms. I guess I have to order them online because I can't go to my local drugstore. I know it sounds like I'm twelve years old, but I don't want everyone to know my business."

Alerts about STDs are not intended to push widows away from sex but, rather, to make sure they are safe while reclaiming physical pleasure. Widows should put themselves through a primer on condoms (with their dizzying array of sizes, colors, flavors), and learn how the small latex or polyurethane sheets, known as dental dams, can be used during oral sex. When unsure about a partner, widows have options beyond traditional intercourse. They include erotic massage; kissing, kissing, and more kissing; mutual masturbation; and phone sex (which is naughty talk).

Other options include "outercourse." Sometimes referred to as dry humping or frottage or even smashing, this is sexual activity that brings pleasure through touch and friction, rather than penetration. It can be done with clothes on or off. In its strictest form, it means no penetration of any kind. A looser interpretation welcomes the use of fingers (or other manual stimulation) and sex toys. The National Women's Health Network has a webpage that discusses outercourse practices and provides other resources for building a creative sex life.[5]

Outercourse isn't a 100 percent safeguard against STDs, but it is lower risk, especially when good hygiene is used. It is also preferred by some couples when erectile dysfunction or painful intercourse (dyspareunia) are challenges.

Like the late cartoonist John Callahan said: "Sex is like air; it's not important unless you aren't getting any." The notion that women lose their sex drive at a certain age or that widows do not need intimacy after bereavement is a myth. A 2017 survey, as part of the University of Michigan National Poll on Healthy Aging, asked a national sample of adults ages sixty-five to eighty about sex. The majority called sex an important part of a romantic relationship at any age.[6] There is no shelf life for libido.

Intimacy today has slipped beyond coitus into an array of more creative areas, and the only rules are the ones a widow feels comfortable with. Physical pleasure is a healthy human need. Connection, the joy of skin-on-skin contact, and satisfying sex are among life's lovely and mystical experiences. There is every reason in the world for widows to reclaim their lust.

FROM MARTI'S BLOG

Breaking In and Out of the Dating (Sex) World

Are you thinking about putting yourself out there after being with the same spouse for one, two, three, or more decades? Keep your expectations somewhat low, but also brace for delights.

I don't want to be too positive or negative here. I know widows who met a great partner right out of the gate, but that is more the exception than the rule. In my case, I waited a year after Tom died and randomly went to a speed-dating session one cold night after work. I figured it would be a new experience, maybe one I could write about.

I didn't realize the magnitude of what I was taking on. After all, only a few months earlier I thought I would never be with another man again, and I was trying to prepare for life alone—forever. But here I was at a micro-brewery trying to avert my eyes from the guys hovering around the bar, feeling nervous and on edge. In fact, I walked out once and sat in my car, ready to bolt. But it was too cold even with the heat on, so I talked myself into going back in. I had nothing to lose.

I finally took a seat at my designated table—No. 5—and, after the first six minutes of asking and answering questions with the first stranger, the nervousness lifted. Heck, it was a lot like interviewing people for news stories, which I had been doing for almost forty years.

So I went with it and talked briefly with eleven more guys. It was fun, and I quickly learned all were divorced except two—who were widowers. One of the widowers had bad teeth. The other enthusiastically encouraged me to choose him. He promised widowhood wisdom since he was two years ahead of me on the dating scene. He also was eight years younger, which appealed to me.

This frivolous escapade led to five months of semi-regular dating with the "choose me" widower. It provided many fraught-with-danger firsts since my husband's death—namely sex and physical affection, sharing a bathroom, observing eating habits, and many, long talks about our spouses, his dating experiences, and our relationship. I have to admit the first time getting naked (in my marital bed) with someone after being with the same guy for more than twenty-eight years was scary, but also exhilarating. I even found his choice of boxer briefs tantalizing and made a mental note that this was what younger men must be wearing these days. I was used to a man who wore briefs and only occasionally boxers.

The exciting experience of dating this guy gave me an escape from grief for a short time and served up comfort and security. But things ended after, out of the blue, he asked if I wanted to be exclusive. I wasn't sure what this meant at the time, and after learning said I was not ready to be exclusive so fast. He did not like this response, got testy and made a crazy switch saying if I didn't want to be exclusive, he was going to start dating other women. (He said early on he was in pursuit of another wife.)

This experience saddened me. We eventually broke up and I did substantial grieving and crying over the next few months. A grief therapist I saw a few times told me when adversity strikes, grief can return.

I decided I had been too trusting and open with this guy and vowed I wouldn't do that again. (But I did it again.)

Since then, I've had a few coffees, phone conversations, and outings with men I've met online. I also had another relationship experience with a guy who, after going out for a couple months, failed to tell me he had a girlfriend on the East Coast. He would disappear for trips to Florida or Boston and I wouldn't hear from him for days. I eventually wised up and broke off all ties with him.

I continue to spend time with my sweeping assortment of friends (mostly women) and family and work to embrace and feel comfortable with my aloneness. But I'll never forget the first guys I was intimate with after my dear husband's death.

· 7 ·

Love Is Not Enough

I fell in love with you because there was a mischief in your eyes.

—French author and journalist Michka Assayas

They have chatted online, perhaps even spoken on the phone, but face to face is where the true test begins. They're meeting for the first time, maybe over coffee or a beer. One of them, let's make it the widow, out of the blue, says something negative about a political leader or takes a stand on a hot-button issue. Her date is not only on the other side of the table, literally, but also across it politically. Does this fledgling relationship have a future?

No. Yes. Maybe.

The compatibility question, which can cover a lot of ground, challenges new couples. In our increasingly polarized world, friendships and romances flourish when people share common ideas and opinions. Sometimes, though, romance can grow amid dissent. How can a widow gauge when a relationship is right for her?

When a young woman pairs up with her high school or college sweetheart and they set off on a life journey, they evolve as a couple, building their values, belief system, and life philosophy together over the years. Their shared adventures help them fine-tune their principles, and their collective perspective keeps the relationship strong. (In fact, people sometimes divorce because that shared worldview splits or comes to loggerheads.)

Widows have gone the long game with their commitment to a relationship. Because of that, they return to the dating world bearing firmly planted ideas—and ideals—that have deepened over time and sharpened through life experiences. These ideas span the spectrum from essential core values to beliefs as mundane as how chores should be divided within a household. The complex interplay among these forces makes some widows anguish about whether it is even conceivable to find a new partner whose outlook matches theirs.

"I met him when he was fourteen. We married when I was twenty-two and he was twenty-four," said Evie, whose husband died unexpectedly. "We worked together and we retired together when he turned sixty. We were happy."

For Evie, the idea of finding someone else seems impossible after having two lives so deeply entwined. She and her husband had agreed on how to live, on where to live, on what they would do together, and on what they would do apart. They had planned a post-work future that embraced all the details that were important to them as a couple. She doubts that can happen a second time.

Gretchen felt differently and, not long after becoming a widow, she found herself in a happy relationship with someone very unlike her husband.

"He is totally opposite from my husband, but we enjoy one another," she said of her companion, who parents in a different style, holds opposite political views, and supports his adult children financially, something she views as enabling. "We travel a great deal and we have other things in common. We both like to go to concerts. We both do a great deal of walking and bicycling and kayaking."

Once, in acknowledgment of their opposing political positions, she went to a Republican Party event with him and he joined her at a gathering of political progressives. "I can tell you, there was room for lots of conversation after that," she said with a laugh. "It was interesting."

For widows, the launch of a new relationship can easily find itself turning into a litmus test of values. Work ethics, standards of respect, religious beliefs, parenting styles, voting records, viewpoints on social issues, and more. A widow might watch her date's reaction to being cut off in traffic, being ignored by a waiter, or seeing an alma mater lose in the Final Four playoffs. How is a new romantic interest when he or she travels, away from their comfort zone and control? Actor Will Ferrell joked that anyone considering marriage should first observe their partner using a slow-speed internet connection. Someone else has suggested the ultimate test of compatibility is whether a couple can successfully assemble IKEA furniture together.

Susanna, whose husband died after a long illness, had a clear idea of what she envisioned in a new partner. "I wanted somebody very intelligent. I see myself as a thinking and questioning person," she said. "I was raised as a Unitarian although, in terms of religion, I get along well with people from a wide variety of religions. But I wanted someone who has similar values—and what I value is human beings, social interactions."

Susanna is an active person. Instead of watching TV, she would rather be out and about, in motion. She was not willing to travel a long geographic distance for romance. "And I knew I didn't want anybody into drinking and smoking," she explained.

Monica, too, said she has a clear idea of the qualities she wants in a man. "I don't know what gift the universe has waiting for me, but I expect any new partner to be independent and physically healthy and active. They also need to be lighthearted and see the humor in things."

What is important in a new partner? Must they be smart, well read, athletic, or active? Do they need an appreciation for culture? A writer might vow never to date anyone who doesn't know the rules of grammar, while a foodie might want someone who has broad tastes in cuisine and expertise in the kitchen. But are those touchstones indispensable? Are they all it takes to keep seeing someone or a reason to walk away? Or should the relationship be underpinned by something broader?

Common or complementary interests and, sometimes, common friends, are what often draw people together. But shared values are what keep the romance going.

Interests are the easy part. Often they are what make paths cross in the first place. Sunday morning strolls through second-hand bookshops or long-distance bike rides. Bargain shopping at estate sales or volunteer work at the local animal rescue. A common interest can involve a fascination with horror movies or a preference for techno music. Shared interests play an important role in bonding a couple, but they are not the foundation of a rich romance. While they bring energy to some relationships, they are optional for others.

Maura, who remains friends with a widower she dated for a few years, said she doesn't think "love is valentines and unicorns," but she had an idea in mind when she met her former boyfriend. She wanted him to be smart and to appreciate theater and art like she does. She wanted him to love books. But he countered that making such "lists" of criteria for a companion was limiting. She said that conversation between them was an important learning moment.

"I have an adopted daughter, which means that once before I took a perfect stranger into my heart and what has come out of that commitment has been so rich and wonderful that I will love her forever," said Maura. "So really, I think now that my definition of love is not about a list of preferences. It's that you care how that other person's story turns out. I think love is a decision you make."

COMMON INTERESTS ARE NOT VALUES

Some people confuse common interests with common values.

People can—and do—find love even with few interests in common. Those couples pop up everywhere: the woman whose passion is dance but her partner can't be dragged to the dance floor, or the bird-watcher whose significant other would rather be at a poetry slam. That's OK. There are more consequential elements to a relationship, among them honesty and respect.

An argument can even be made that a romance constructed disproportionately upon common interests may falsely prolong its shelf life because it keeps people busy with shared activities while obscuring deeper needs or problems. The other thing about shared interests is that they shift—and not always in tandem. Someone devoted for years to art classes may suddenly find that environmental issues hold greater importance for them. Concert-going may be abandoned and replaced with travel. Weight loss can spark greater affinity for athletic activities while a move to a seaside community can convert a landlubber into a boater.

Aging and injuries also can play devilish tricks on common interests. There may come a time when physical changes wean one member of a couple away from the rock-climbing or kayaking weekends they both loved so much. Those are not the kinds of shifts that should bring a relationship to an end. In a solid romance, when interests change or evaporate, the values that unite a couple will still be there.

Common interests add dimension to a relationship. Shared values, on the other hand, tie down the foundation of a successful relationship. Passion, integrity, financial stability, kindness, and success may be values for some widows. So, too, are honesty, loyalty, frugality, a belief in a healthy work-life balance, the pursuit of pleasure, or a commitment to those in need.

Shared interests, of course, may be an outward expression of values. Take the couple who met at the dog park. Their common interest in canines may reflect core beliefs about how animals should be treated. Similarly, the culinary preferences of two vegetarians may signal that they put a premium on the pursuit of good health, or that they share a spiritual philosophy that calls for living in harmony with the natural world.

Values are the beliefs that define who a person is and provide consistency in life. They help establish rules, determine choices made, influence reactions to moral dilemmas, and set boundaries. In simplistic terms, values are what help individuals decide what is right and what is wrong.

For widows like Susanna, there were desired targets—in both thought and action—for a healthy romance. "I wouldn't go out with someone who splurged and spent all their money frivolously. I wouldn't date someone who is not a good money manager," she said. "I also care about things like the environment. That is one of the general values that I have."

Widows—like all people who navigate grief—are changed by their losses. Their interests may fluctuate, their priorities may readjust. Still, their deepest-held values usually remain intact. And that is both important and challenging for new romances. The crucial thing for widows to remember when looking for a new partner is that they do not have to find someone whose *every* value matches theirs. Romance can flourish even amid dissent and differences. Remember the old adage about opposites and attraction? Often it is enough to be aligned on points that hold the greatest weight.

ON THE TESTING GROUND

The lists are everywhere—in newspapers, magazines, and blogs—enumerating the qualities a woman should watch for in a new romantic partner or, alternatively, qualities that are deal-breakers. As Maura discovered, the list game is a limiting one. By singling out the Top Ten qualities desired in a new partner and requiring that every one is checked off, a widow risks missing the bigger picture. Human beings are complex creatures with delightful, intriguing, and often contradictory behaviors and positions.

So, while the values debate sounds simple enough at first glance, it can be a conundrum. Some relationship gurus counsel couples to break away from the deal-buster mentality by thinking positively. Rather than envisioning what will not be tolerated, they suggest imagining what is especially desired in a romantic partner. To undertake this exercise, a widow might deeply consider her values—and honestly examine why she holds them—and then ask what they mean for her in a relationship. If, for example, she values work-life balance, how will she deal with someone who is a workaholic? It may be that she and her new partner share the same value, a strong work ethic, but that she places a higher premium on another value: a strong commitment to family and friends.

Couples' retreats incorporate exercises to help people plumb what is important to them individually and jointly. Widows and their new partners might even test their compatibility through online question-naires designed to show where they align and where they are mis-matched. These are not scientific but they can spark interesting and enlightening conversations. There is even a cottage industry—value coaching—that has emerged to help individuals and couples examine their life philosophies.

Of course, a widow may choose to sidestep the values category al-together and, instead, gravitate toward light fun with no strings attached. Think bad boys with buff bods. The widow may get nothing more than a series of one-night stands, but that can be OK, too. Not all dating has to launch a long-term relationship. If fun in the bedroom is all a widow is seeking right now, then more power to her.

GAUGING WHEN THERE IS ALIGNMENT

Honesty is critical for Andrew, who was in his thirties when his wife died. Like Maura, he now has a broad perspective about what he wants in a partner. "I can take various attributes that seem to sum up to 'be-ing open-minded,'" he explained. "I think I feel most comfortable with someone who is curious about the world and not too judgmental about what is happening around them.

"Of course, there are key values you have to agree on. Do you want to live a life of crime? Are you abusive or do you think abusive behavior is beneficial? But those are the really basic things that you pick up from observations and from cues, and those are the first line for deciding if you want to consider a relationship," he said. "Beyond that point comes the real discovery, getting to know a person for who they are."

Andrew's first marriage was marked by contrasts. He and his wife were of different races, raised in separate cultures, and living together in a highly polarized urban area. "She didn't see the world exactly as I saw it because she didn't have the same experiences I had, but she was open-minded and asked questions about who I am. And that was the key to our relationship," he said.

"You look for commonality when you meet someone," he continued. "You have a conversation about a book you've both read or a movie you've both seen. Or maybe you're a fan of Duke Ellington and they're a fan of Duke Ellington and you both like to go to art museums. But for me, those things are not the ultimate deciding factor."

For many others, however, there *are* benchmarks—in both thought and action—that are drivers of a healthy romance. They surface as both things in common, such as interests and activities, and areas where there is divergence.

BATTLEGROUNDS: RELIGION AND POLITICS

There are core beliefs that shape people. Chief among them today in the United States are religion and politics.

For some people, religious compatibility is as important as sexual compatibility. Several studies have found that shared religious beliefs can translate into stronger relationship commitment and more success in maintaining a relationship.[1] However, this research focuses primarily on people who are already married. A University of Nebraska study that looked at religion in the context of dating among young adults found that romances were more satisfying if religious beliefs were shared. Interestingly, the research also found that shared religious beliefs did not necessarily lead to *long-term* commitment.[2] Even more, the Pew Research Center has concluded that with each generation, religion is becoming less important, including in the United States, Canada, and most of Latin America.[3]

Studies aside, religion can be a very personal issue. Christian, Jewish, Muslim? If the other values are shared, people may compromise when it comes to religious congruence, which generations back was often imperative. Today, new partners may use simpler standards: How does this new partner treat others? Is this person kind and generous?

"He is more religious than I am. He's one of the people who goes to church on the holy days he's supposed to," said widow Gretchen, whose relationship is strong despite a long roster of differences. "I don't go with him. But that's all right."

For a year, Katie, divorced, dated a widower who is Jewish. He wanted to remarry. "When we talked about marriage, he asked if I'd be willing to convert to Judaism. I told him I didn't have any religion so I didn't care one way or another," she said. "For me, the more important thing is that we discovered our values were so similar. Even though I come from a country life and he came from a city life, we had evolved in a compatible way."

Although Katie's relationship with the widower did not last, religion was not the problem point. Rather, he could not move through his grief in a healthy way.

Religion may be a factor in finding a partner, but politics in recent years has emerged as a much stronger force thanks to a highly divisive political landscape in the United States. Gretchen and her longtime companion have figured out how to rise above their differences. She is a flaming liberal while her boyfriend tends toward conservatism. "But that's OK as he is less emotional than me," she said. They don't share political views, but they have other shared interests, such as watersports and art, that they value.

There are high-profile examples of public figures whose political divergences are legendary, yet their politically mixed marriages survive. Kellyanne Conway, a former operative in Donald Trump's White House, and her husband George Conway, a vociferous critic of the Trump presidency, are a prime example. Democratic strategist James Carville and his wife Mary Matalin, who does the same kind of work but for Republicans, have been together for more than two decades. However, recent research has found that being in sync on US politics has become more and more essential for people seeking romantic partners.

After the election of 2016, a study by dating site eharmony found that nearly half its users had mentioned Donald Trump in their profiles (both positively and negatively). Around the same time, dating websites like TrumpSingles, ConservativesOnly, and RepublicanSinglesDating started popping up. Dating website Bumble added a feature in 2018 that allowed users to share their political party preferences, and 40 percent of its users took advantage of the tool.

US political and social divisiveness has put a terrible strain on relationships. Findings from the American Perspectives Survey in January 2020 indicated that most people do not identify a single issue that would be a deal-breaker for them when dating, but political differences make dating more difficult.[4] Survey respondents were specifically asked about hot-button issues such as climate change, gun control, LGBTQ+ rights, immigration, and racial discrimination. Only a small segment of respondents said they would never date someone on the other side of the issue. And a big chunk of survey respondents claimed they could nourish a romance with someone with opposite views. With one exception: abortion.

"The religion piece doesn't matter to me. Politics don't matter to me. I'm a vegetarian, but the person I date doesn't have to be a vegetarian," said Margaret, who was widowed four years ago. "I can imagine having fun sparring over some of those things.

"But abortion is important. I am pro-choice and at the end of the day I want to be with someone who believes that all people should have the opportunity to be what they want to be," she added.

In the American Perspectives Survey, no subject proved to be a bigger deal-breaker than abortion. A quarter of the respondents said it would be impossible for them to date anyone who was not in alignment with them on abortion. Another 44 percent said it would be very or somewhat difficult.

When asked about whether they would date someone with differing religious views, meanwhile, the respondents' answers hinged largely on the religious beliefs they embraced. A majority of white evangelical Christians said they would not date anyone with different religious beliefs. Only 8 percent of atheists said religious views would make a difference. Catholics and mainstream Christians said it would be a factor but not an overriding one.

PILLARS OF A SUCCESSFUL RELATIONSHIP

What makes a relationship work? It's hard to imagine a question that engenders more far-flung answers.

A German physicist who does a stand-up comedy routine in New York maintains that the key to a lasting relationship is as simple as a shared sense of humor. One relationship expert cited trust, commitment, and vulnerability while another underscored a combination of interdependence and independence. A research study at Ohio State University found that while all couples face conflict in their relationships, how successfully they handled them was heavily impacted by a single factor: whether they were getting enough sleep.[5] (The most hostile couples were the ones who were shuteye deprived.) In other research, good communication emerges as a pivotal factor.

Compatibility does not mean agreement on everything. Nor does compatibility grow out of conflict avoidance. That's why smart relationships include a strategy for fighting. More elegantly put, it is important to plan for disagreement, to think about how to cope with conflict, and to learn how to negotiate. Unproductive arguing can become entrenched, whittling away at relationships. People—even those who are wildly in love—need to know how to say what needs to be said, even when it is difficult.

How does a widow launch a productive conversation about something uncomfortable? There are plenty of advice mantras. She could ask her partner if it's a good time to talk; set her sights on solving the problem, not one-upping or launching into a monologue; be empathetic but make sure she is clear on her own needs; acknowledge anger but choose not to indulge it. Many of these are skills a widow likely had in her last relationship. She just needs to bring them forward, maybe with modifications, with her new partner.

Differences, meanwhile, are meant to be acknowledged, honored, and, when necessary, accommodated. A widow might like a clean house and believe in an equal division of labor. Her partner could be more casual about cleanup and gleaming floors. If they have the resources, they could hire a cleaning service. Conflict solved. What if a widow likes time alone, but her partner loves being with her, talking with her, inhabiting the same room she is in? The couple could address this by drawing up guidelines that ensure both of them get the time they need—together and apart. Some things, of course, are not so easy. That's where compromise comes in. Everyone gives a little.

There will be impasses. Some people have deeply embedded, even cringeworthy, traits that are unlikely to change. Take the tightwad. Or what about the hoarder?

Nearly everyone we spoke with for this book mentioned the importance of honesty. Can a relationship be built without honesty? Most people returning to love after a death are willing to trust people who haven't earned it yet. They are willing to take that chance, especially widows who have been in relationships that were solid on honesty. That's human nature. That's how love begins.

In fact, honesty might be the biggest value. As people come to know a new romantic partner, they talk about their life, loves, children, jobs, passions. They may not reveal all at once, but they hope that each story that unfolds, good or bad, is true. Honesty not only exposes flaws, it unveils strengths. It makes people seem more human. It also nourishes trust, the Holy Grail of solid love.

Of course, even the most honest soul may occasionally lie or mislead. However, one of the worst experiences is to be honest and open with someone only to find out the relationship has been underpinned by lies. Heartbreaking, a scenario like this might make a widow want to pull out of the dating game—perhaps for good. However, survival in the dating world is all about resiliency and the ability to pop back up after being knocked down.

FROM MARTI'S BLOG

Know When to Walk Away

I met, let's call him Bill, online. After a few weeks of emailing and a long phone conversation, we met for coffee downtown. I wasn't sure what to make of him, but I had the coincidence of knowing a woman who knows him and she gave him a ringing endorsement.

He was older than me by six years—the oldest man I've gone out with—a retired cop, politically conservative, sexually liberal, brimming with contradictions. He loved urban bike riding, socializing, and supporting his hometown to a fault.

He smelled good and chewed gum all the time so there was never a hint of foul breath. He seemed to like me a lot.

After hours of conversations, with me asking about his past relationships and experiences, I became suspect. So many of my questions, especially about past romances, were not answered. I was told repeatedly that maybe someday he'd tell me. Meanwhile, I was my open-book self.

He kept leaving town for his condo in Florida or on business trips where he claimed to be teaching classes to other law enforcement professionals. I wouldn't hear much from him when he was gone, but when he came back, he was all over me. I was frustrated but found myself strongly attracted to him. I told him how I felt and frequently complained about his lack of openness and reluctance to make weekend plans. Everything had to be spontaneous.

He was very different than me, but one day he brought up that although we were different, we shared values. This made me feel better, and I agreed with him. I liked the sound of that comment.

After coming back from an unusually long trip without much communication, he came over and coyly told me he had been visiting his girlfriend of twenty years, who was now just a good friend. Yes, they sleep together but don't have sex. ("Oh brother . . ." I can hear all my friends say.) Reportedly, he's not attracted to her anymore. She meets him at his condo in Florida, too. Oh yeah, she and his sister are close. What? I was blown away. It was clear that this guy was bad news.

I should have walked away after that confession. He presented himself as a single man, but he wasn't. Foolishly, I stayed on as a friend of sorts, but the unfulfilled chemistry between us was painful. His vacations with his "friend" were hurtful, yet I continued to meet him for bike rides or dinner. Four months of this passed before I severed every tie with him. I never communicated with him again. The whole episode left me hurt and sad. I still look back with regret that I didn't end it quicker. Clearly, our values were night and day.

Traveling with an Entourage

I have to accept the fact that, no matter what I do, it's going to annoy someone.

—Actor Nathan Lane

*I*t is a rare widow who does not have people who are interested in how her life unfolds. These people—her entourage—often rise up as a widow's most powerful support during grief. They may also become the most persistent obstacles in her journey to new love.

When two people forge a romance, they bring together their tribes, from parents and siblings to friends and colleagues. Blended families are already a common part of marriage in the United States. However, when one person in the new relationship is a widow, there are additional, and elaborate, layers of people to wade past while dating, among them in-laws. The full entourage may include friends of the deceased spouse; long-time neighbors; pets; babysitters; and even sports, theater, book-reading, or [fill-in-the-blank] social buddies. That's a lot of people to offer support to a new romance. It can also be a formidable throng if its members decide to go judgmental.

People in the entourage inevitably carry their own grief. And their loyalties. How do you spell l-a-n-d-m-i-n-e?

Widows reclaiming a romantic life are often surprised by the push-back they get from those closest to them. One widow we talked to received it from her granddaughter; several women faced it from their children. New relationships can be unsettling for offspring who feel their deceased parent is being replaced. Some fear they will be assigned a lesser role in their mother's life, that their mother will be hurt somehow, or even that their inheritance will be diluted or diverted. For in-laws, meanwhile, it may feel like a new romance is erasing their deceased child or they may worry that a new relationship will interfere with their connection and access to grandchildren.

Friends, meanwhile, may heft their protective shields, convinced their widow friend will fall victim to a dating app scam if they are not safeguarded. Sometimes jealousy, subconsciously, rears its head. If the widow is involved with a new partner, will the friends who have supported her through her grief be sidelined? If they were friends of both the widow and her deceased partner, they may feel that there is a betrayal. They, too, are grieving and new romance may feel like too much, too soon. They are, perhaps naturally, thinking about their feelings rather than the loneliness of the widow.

Sometimes it's not even about the widow dating. It's about misinterpreting a widow's role or falling into yesteryear stereotypes about behavior and intention.

"We had a neighbor who was always over at our house with my husband, helping him on projects," Isabella said. "One day, after my husband died, I was out at the curb talking to the neighbor when his wife came out and said, 'Are you flirting with my husband?'

"I had always seen this woman as my friend, and I was pissed off and hurt that she would say something like that to me. The reality is that there are some women who feel threatened by widows, and that makes me sad," Isabella said.

Widows occasionally are shocked and hurt, too, when their friends' husbands make a pass. One woman said a male friend at her husband's funeral told her she was "the hottest widow in the room."

The reactions of those in a widow's circle are important for many reasons, but two are pivotal. After the death of a spouse, a woman may become more sensitive to what people think and advise. At the same time, strong social support can influence the quality of a widow's new relationship.

OFFSPRING FORM THE FRONT LINE

In love-after-death scenarios, children usually rear up as the greatest challenge. Regardless of their age, a widow's offspring have been knocked flat by loss and grief. As they work through that unthinkable life experience, they may try to monitor the behavior of a parent who is beginning to date. Any relationships involving their mother may signal (to their mind, anyway) that their deceased parent is being forgotten. They don't want a substitute for an absent parent.

Gretchen was widowed at age fifty-nine after a long, happy marriage. Her companion was divorced for six years before they launched their romance. Gretchen harbored no illusions about merging her family with that of her boyfriend. "I have one child, but we have a difficult relationship, always have. My daughter has two children I am close to," she explained. Her partner has three grown children, one of whom has a troubled life.

"The result is we do not have family relationships together," she said. "He sees my grandchildren once a week or so when they're over and I see his, but our families are not joined." The couple is content with this workaround.

Of course, some widows find the process of merging families to be a happy one. That was Susanna's experience when she began a new relationship. Susanna's husband died when she was fifty-six. A widow for more than a dozen years now, she brought two grown daughters and their families—including young grandchildren—to her current relationship. Her companion, who is divorced, has a daughter and two grandchildren. "We've meshed our families," Susanna said. "We do holidays together. At Christmas time, his grandkids stay here."

Susanna said her partner doesn't have other close family members nearby, "but I've met his family and I love his sisters. We have a great time together." She noted that he travels with her to visit her mother.

That dovetailing of families worked almost seamlessly until those yours-mine-our loyalties were tested with a death. The funeral for the father of Susanna's partner fell on the same day as her granddaughter's much-awaited birthday party. Susanna and her partner brainstormed until they found a compromise.

"I went for the birthday then rushed back in time for the funeral and was with his family," she said. "We accommodate each other."

There is some common ground when widows with children launch romances with divorced parents who have children. Collectively, these offspring have all undergone a displacement sparked by the end of a marriage, albeit one through death and the other through a divorce. There is a mutual opportunity to build a new family that supports everyone. This can be true even when the "children" are grown.

Katie envisioned a richer family life through her romance with a widower. She had ended a long marriage as her two daughters reached college age. After some searching, she began dating a widower whose daughter was not long out of college. This young woman had only been eight years old when her mother died, and she was not used to her father dating. But she liked Katie's daughters.

"We had the girls all here for spring break a few months after we began our relationship. The five of us. I thought it would go very easily, and it did. The girls all got along," Katie said. "His daughter is a lot like mine, in the same realm of intelligence and with the same manners and values. And at this age, these kids were never all going to live together under the same roof, so that makes it easier.

"I think he wanted me to be in a motherly role for his daughter and I was willing to do that. I like her. It was really easy for me to be with her," Katie explained. "As for my girls, he reached out to them. I thought he could have been more of a father figure to them than their own father.

"And for all our daughters, who have been through divorce and death, we provided the example of a healthy relationship."

This family clicked, but only for a while. And when it did hit rough waters, it wasn't because of the children but because of other obstacles Katie and her partner were unable to resolve together.

Louise, who fell in love again with a long-ago sweetheart after her husband's death, has three sons in their thirties. Two welcomed the news that she had launched a new relationship. Not so with the youngest son. "He isn't jumping up and down. He was very connected to his father. I also think he's afraid I will get hurt," she said.

Parents have separate relationships with each of their children. These individual relationships continue after a spouse dies, even if a widow adds another person to her life. How that new person influences a widow's decisions is important to offspring. The complex dynamics of families, joined with the complex dynamics of new love, can spawn problems—both real and perceived.

There is a real concern, certainly, that the children of young widows be ensured the constancy they need when their mother is busy dating. And a forty-something woman has a legitimate grievance when her stepfather launches a romance just a month after her mother's un-expected death. The "too soon" benchmark can be applied to family members just as easily as it can to the widows themselves.

Andrew was widowed two decades ago when he was in his late thirties, and that loss continues to mark his life. His stepdaughter Naomi was twenty-two when her mother died; at the time, Naomi was in-volved with the man who would eventually become her husband.

"I'm always thinking about Naomi and her growing family as part of my life," Andrew said. "She had already gone to college and was starting her own life when her mother died, and I didn't expect her to remain close to me. I thought that as time went on, she might see me as someone who made her remember her mother, as a trigger of grief.

"But that's not what happened at all. Naomi and I became closer. And that caused a complication with new relationships because I always wondered, 'What will Naomi think? Will she think I'm trying to replace her mother or not honoring her mother's memory?'"

Andrew dated off and on for several years after his wife's death, then entered a deeper, cross-country romance that lasted nearly a de-cade. Ironically, that union ended shortly after he and his long-time girlfriend finally decided to marry. He said that making it "official" somehow widened the gap that already existed between the new bride and groom and their relationships with each other's children.

For one thing, the chemistry between his second wife and Naomi was not good. "I think Naomi was too much of a reminder of that first marriage," he said of the wife's disputes with his stepdaughter. "At the same time, I think Naomi was being protective of me."

He also found it difficult to build a relationship with his new wife's children, whom he described as coddled and dismissive of the values he embraced. An emotional wall started to take shape. Eventually it proved too high to scale and the marriage did not last long. Andrew then became involved for a few years with a younger woman who had no children. Naomi and the new girlfriend got along fantastically.

TAKE MY IN-LAWS. PLEASE.

In-laws can be tricky beasts. They share a history with the widow (and her children, if there are any). If it's a long and close relationship, they may continue to influence behaviors and decisions. And they may have a complicated posthumous relationship with their deceased son or daughter.

Like the widow, these people have been through a gut-wrenching loss. They may consciously or unconsciously feel that their offspring is being usurped when their daughter-in-law dates. They might worry about how this new romance will affect their contact with their daughter-in-law and grandchildren. They may see nothing but storms on the horizon.

"My relationships with friends and family changed when my wife passed away. There was more distance between us. Eventually, there wasn't much contact with any of her friends or her family," said one widower. "But I have to tell you, if someone had ever said, 'If your wife dies, would you continue to have a relationship with her family?' my answer would have correctly been, 'Yes, but not much of a relationship.'"

In contrast, Detroit executive Jack, a widower for seven years who has been dating a divorced woman for three years, remains tight with his deceased wife's family, as do his children. "After my wife died, my in-laws, who lived in Cleveland, came and stayed with me and the kids for six months," he said. They helped care for his children, allowing him to deal with his grief and dramatic life change.

A sixty-three-year-old construction company executive has ended up with a less-than-close relationship with her in-laws, but it is not for lack of trying. She worked to forge a relationship, but the family remained resentful, blaming her for breaking up his prior marriage years earlier, an accusation she strongly denied. She married for the first time in her early fifties; her husband died when they were both fifty-eight. She tries not to worry about how new relationships might affect her in-laws.

Margaret, a younger widow with children, has the full support not only of her parents, siblings, and friends but also that of her in-laws as she looks for a new partner. She wants to make sure that any new beau understands she and her family come together as a package deal.

"I love my family, as quirky as they are, and my extended family, as quirky as it is, too," Margaret said. "It's important to me that the person who comes into my life also likes them. I can't envision, for example, getting remarried and not having them all there, my in-laws, all of my extended family."

Even with in-laws who show respect and grace when a new romantic partner appears, old habits and family rituals die hard. Sometimes the toll is not on the widow but on her new partner. Take the case of a multigenerational group with a widower at the center. (It could just as easily have been a widow.) When the family came together at the holidays with his father-in-law, the patriarch of the clan, the gathering included sons, their spouses, and children; the spouses' parents; and great grandparents. Also joining the extended family event was the widower's girlfriend. They had been dating for a few years.

Someone called for photos to document the event. First the great grandparents posed with their great-grandchildren, followed by various combinations of offspring, before multiple generations from each family lined up before the camera. Throughout, the widower's girlfriend stood on the sidelines watching. She had no family role. She was neither a parent nor grandparent. She was never called and, in the end, she appeared in none of the photos.

How should widows and their new partners navigate the in-law landscape? The answer to that question depends a great deal on the depth of the in-law relationship, although it is always a good idea to introduce the new partner. Too often a widow sets up an unnecessary obstacle course out of some misguided worry that her new romance will hurt her in-laws. By cross-pollinating family gatherings and celebrations with *everyone*, tension can be defused. Many widows suggested that in-laws be included until, and unless, the dynamics become toxic.

In-laws are not the only ones who can interfere with new relationships. A widow's parents may also be disapproving, especially if they had a tight connection with the deceased spouse.

Ultimately, the goal is to be realistic. If a widow tries to merge her new life with her old one and she is forced over and over again to choose sides, it is okay to say "enough" and follow her happiness.

FRIENDSHIPS: TRICKY TO BLEND?

Friends can also be a forbidding landscape to maneuver. Research shows that, over time, couples tend to pair up with other couples as friends. Sometimes they even set up standing social commitments, a movie every other Saturday or a double-date at New Year's. When one member of the foursome dies, the dynamic is thrown off. The surviving partner is likely to find herself slipping (or even being nudged) outside the orbit of the remaining couples.

There are friends who maintain the widow needs "more time" before socializing again, or they keep a distance because they don't know what to say or do. (Death is a reminder that no relationship is safe, and that can be a hard reality for friends to digest.) Even when friends stay in touch, the changed life widowhood brings—singleness or a new companion or a series of new dates—alters the old, predictable group dynamic. As time passes, widows may hear less from their network.

The widower Katie dated didn't have friends and was estranged from his only brother. "He said that when his wife died, many of his friends didn't know how to handle a relationship with him without her. He felt abandoned by his friends," she said. "I have a great community of friends and I wanted him to get integrated into it. He met some of my friends. But when we were together, I worried that I was his everything because he didn't have his own support system."

Time also may be a factor. As people become used to being single, they may realize that being single also means more freedom to cultivate new friendships. Couples are sometimes boxed in by the preferences of one or the other of the partners. And there's always the question of whether the friendships of single people, a less complicated dynamic than group friendships, are somehow more enduring.

That said, when widows lose their partners, they also lose the messy noise and laughter (and drama) that accompanied their relationship. The people generating this energy may not have been the widow's pals, but they were in her life. With these and other friends calling less often, Saturday nights alone can be miserable. And that can be a reminder to widows of the importance of rebuilding their social safety nets.

There is another dynamic that surfaces when end-of-life care for a dying spouse eats up the energy that would otherwise have nurtured friendships. Many widows in this situation emerge from bereavement facing solitude simply because they did not have the bandwidth to care for their sick spouse *and* fuel vibrant friendships.

"As his illness progressed, my husband and I didn't socialize as much," said Susanna, whose husband died of leukemia. "Instead, it became all about family. We would take a family vacation, we would go to visit family, and we would do things around the house together.

"I was working full time. I still had kids. I was trying to deal with his illness. I just didn't feel I had time to socialize with friends," she explained. "I might have had a women's night out every six weeks or so, but that was it."

When Susanna met her new romantic partner, she turned the friend-less status into a positive, recognizing that she came unencumbered. And remember Gretchen, the widow who did not attempt to merge families with her new partner? She has held fast to her friends and the routines she had with them.

"I refuse to change some things. You keep what you had, even at the holidays," she said. "I still see old friends the day before Christmas. It's blocked out for them."

Friends may appear to disapprove of a widow dating or deepening a new relationship when, in fact, they simply don't know how to act. The best way to safeguard their friendship is by asking widows about their new romances, by respecting a widow's need to be sexually active again, and by putting the widow's feelings ahead of their own—even though it may be hard for them.

There is no set pattern to how, or how smoothly, new people become part of a widow's entourage. Social support can play a role in the quality of a relationship, and couples who meet through friends, school, church, sports, or other close-knit groups often are better supported than those who meet through online dating. Nonetheless, new romantic partners are in uncharted waters. Partnerships that come with offspring who have suffered loss require time and patience. For that matter, the drama and tension may not all unfold on the widow's side of the fence. People who date widows bring their own baggage, such as too-involved ex-spouses. Sometimes the "ex" hovers in the background or, at worst, tries to occupy the stage front and center.

"He has an ex-wife that is still very much in his business," one widow lamented of the man who was divorced six years before she started dating him. She and her companion have been together for five years but the former wife remains a regular presence, even though the man's children are adults.

If faced with opposition to her new relationship, a widow's best approach is to remember that her needs and desires count.

DEFUSING THE GRIEF POLICE

In her book *Option B*, Facebook COO Sheryl Sandberg, best known for her "lean-in" strategy to advance women in business, has written about picking up her life after her husband collapsed and died in 2015. Widowed at forty-seven, she found—among other things—that women are judged more harshly than men when they begin dating after bereavement. Although her brother-in-law helped set her up with a man she eventually married, she was viciously trolled online when she started dating ten months after her husband died.[1] Fortunately, Sandberg's mother-in-law was outspoken in her support of the new romance.

A widow's life, like everyone's, is full of choices that others will second guess. When a person exits from mourning to find happiness again, there is inevitably someone in a widow's circle who feels that it is too soon to re-partner or that dating is disrespectful to the deceased. Some wrongheaded people think one life mate is enough. Others assume the patronizing position that bereavement has made the widow or widower incapable of making decisions, or that the new partner isn't good enough.

People who find themselves romantically entangled with widows or widowers may also be surprised when *their* friends and families go into protective mode, underscoring the perceived downsides of entering a relationship with someone marked by loss.

Most of these grief police have good intentions. Often these grief police will be wrong.

Friends before, during, and after widowhood are a widow's greatest asset. They will help a surviving spouse get through bleak days and weeks. It's only natural for friends to sing the praises of the missing spouse, but it is just as important that they do not elevate the late spouse as competition to the new romance. A widow can run interference on this by being respectful while steering the conversation away from discussion of the past. A post-bereavement romantic partner needs to establish himself or herself as the new person in the circle, not as a substitute for the person who died.

What goes on within marriages is only really clear to those in the marriages. The needs that surface once a marriage is cut short are also very personal. Widows may have to tap stockpiles of resolve to avoid guilt trips. They also must be careful not to self-censor, changing their behavior in advance to avoid criticism. The best defense is often no defense.

Nurturing a new love takes energy. That energy is most productively spent creating and enjoying shared adventures and traditions. (That's why, even when widows work to keep their old holiday traditions and the familiar comfort they represent, they also should add fresh elements that have nothing to do with the absent spouse.)

A successful romance is about loving well. The merger of families and friends can be a delicate undertaking, but it can also end in great joy as a new "community" is cobbled together with love.

FROM MARTI'S BLOG

Nights Out with the Boys—My Husband's Boys

For all our married years, Tom and I had scores of nights out together, but we also had nights out separately. I went out with girlfriends—to bars, movies, outings he had no interest in—while he went out with his guy friends. This worked well; it might not work for everyone, but it was healthy for our marriage.

His nights out were called Boys Night Out, or BNOs. He had a couple of good buddies and their nights out had a format: check out a new bar somewhere nearby or downtown and end the night at a friend of ours' downtown bar that features live music most nights of the week. (Or, at least, I think this is what they did.) Sometimes I'd hear about his nights and I'd share anything interesting about how I spent my night.

After Tom died, his "boys" would sometimes invite me along on their BNOs. (Of all Tom's friends, these were the only ones I heard from after his death.) My first year as a widow, I went out with them every couple of months and it made me feel loved and comforted. Oddly enough, it provided a connection to Tom, and I think my presence, in some odd way, provided them with the same thing.

They included me in their Friday or Saturday frolics just like I was one of the boys. We had good conversation and drinks at new downtown spots. We'd go hear a band at a young, hipster bar. They didn't stray far from my side when we went to our friend's bar. They'd buy me drinks and we'd shoot the shit with each other and regular bar patrons they knew. Our friend, the owner, would give us a bit of his time. I liked their subtle protectiveness at that point in my grief.

The second year I was asked out less by the boys, but that was OK. I started dating someone and felt it was time not to be so protected. When I stopped dating, I started thinking about how I might join the boys for a BNO and meet someone new. But, honestly, I wasn't comfortable with that around them and didn't venture far from their fun-loving sides.

This year, the outings are rarer, but I had a recent enjoyable BNO. I met the guys at a local bar because I didn't want to stay as late as they do. We shared laughs, and the warmth was still there.

I hope we keep this going; I need an occasional BNO. Not only is it good to have male buddies I'm comfortable with, but there's a little piece of Tom in those guys, and I don't want to ever let that go.

· 9 ·

In Sickness and in Health

It's one thing to show your love for someone when everything is going fine and life is smooth. But when the "in sickness and in health" part kicks in and sickness does enter your lives, you're tested. Your resilience is tested.

—Patti Davis, actor and author of *The Long Goodbye*

For six years, Susanna cared for her husband as a progressive disease whittled away at his health. After his death, she was surprised to find herself struggling with health challenges of her own. Her spine went out of alignment. She was grinding her teeth. She had a car accident. Rachel, meanwhile, had fallen a year behind on all her doctor appointments as her husband struggled with what would be a fatal brain tumor. "Every time I went to the doctor after his death, I had high blood pressure," she said. "I was also seeing a psychologist because my anxiety level was so high. I would be out running errands and feel OK, then I would suddenly freak out. I almost had an accident a couple of times and became very frightened by these panic attacks."

Monica, too, found her health less than optimum after her partner's death. She struggled to control her diabetes, and her cholesterol shot up. "I had gained weight. I broke my ankle and had a blood clot from that," Monica said. "But more than anything, it was my emotional health that suffered." As her longtime partner's condition deteriorated, she had to deal with his growing frustration and anger.

Health challenges, including many that arise during bereavement, leave a deep imprint on the lives of widows. Marriage and its demise are so intertwined with health that the US Census Bureau does not house widowhood and divorce statistics. Rather, they are the purview of the

National Center for Health Statistics at the CDC. They are considered a public health matter.

Once widows start dating again, they may find themselves tiptoeing around the issue of health. Often it's because health and illness are connected to two of their biggest fears: the dread that they may enter a relationship where they, once again, end up being the caregiver for someone and, simultaneously, the worry that they may be hit with a devastating medical diagnosis that they will have to face alone.

Mental health and physical health are core components in any relationship. However, people who have lost a life partner face three important questions even as they try to build new romantic connections:

1. In what ways has the death of my partner jeopardized my physical and mental health?
2. How am I handling those personal health challenges now that I am single, and in what ways will they affect a new romance?
3. How did my partner's death change my relationship with doctors, illness, recuperation, and caregiving?

Well-being, to a large degree, is how a woman perceives her life is going. It can encompass work, family, financial stability, and other elements, but it is anchored by mind and body health. We know widows are resilient. Research has proven it. But that resilience is not universal. Many of those left behind by death find themselves struggling, mentally and physically. Health can be a high hurdle on the obstacle course left by a partner's death, especially in the early months of widowhood. Health becomes one more layer to manage when trying to date again.

I THINK I'M LOSING MY MIND

Mental health is remarkably complex. For widows, it often encompasses two big challenges: loneliness and depression. Loneliness inevitably accompanies loss. First, a spouse is no longer in the woman's life. Then, in some cases, friends become scarce. They may disappear because they struggle with how to provide support or they flee from anything that reminds them of their mortality. They may be grieving. In other cases, friends may see the widow testing the world of dating and beginning new connections that are distant to them. They don't recognize that friendship and social interaction are a wellness life jacket for widows.

Social isolation carries a serious price, including for widows. Some medical practitioners go so far as to describe loneliness as a scourge or modern-day epidemic. Indeed, loneliness has become so common in our tech-heavy society that the United Kingdom in 2018 even named a position, dubbed by the media as the "Minister of Loneliness," within the government's cabinet.[1] Of course, widows are not the only people navigating loneliness. COVID-19 plunged entire nations into isolation. However, loneliness can be especially hard for widows because they are not used to being on their own.

Loneliness can also be dangerous for widows. A study out of Denmark found that women who were lonely not only had a lower quality of life, but they were three times as likely to suffer anxiety and depression. Loneliness was also a strong predictor of premature death.[2] Other research confirms the link between grief and depression. The depression may be low-grade, or it may be full-blown. It is often persistent. A study involving more than seventy thousand middle-aged women found that first-year widows in the sample faced a significant decline in mental health, although they bounced back over time.[3]

One widower told us he felt ready to date more than a year after the death of his wife of thirty-plus years. He found a romantic partner and energetically embarked on a blissful new relationship. But his friends and family worried that he still looked unhappy. His smiles were rare and muted. His "resting face" was a serious one. He was astonished when a health professional diagnosed him with depression while noting that he probably had been suffering from it ever since his wife's death. In interviews for this book, we found widows who remain on antidepressants for years after the death of a spouse.

Grief runs deep. Grief runs long. Since active social lives may be one of the most effective ways to keep the darkest days at bay, widows who had insular marriages may face the longest recovery. That revelation should raise no eyebrows. What many people don't understand is how staggering grief—and its impact—can be for young widows. Grief affects young widows disproportionately.[4] They are more likely to lose their spouses suddenly, with little time to prepare for the loss, and support resources are typically geared toward older women. Young widows are also more likely to be oddities in their social circles. Their friends don't understand what they are going through; some have never dealt with close death before. At the same time, a spouse's death disrupts a young widow's day-to-day life in myriad ways. Especially if she is working while raising children, she no longer has a partner to split household and childcare responsibilities. She is likely to face deep financial challenges.

The process of bereavement can also be difficult for widows who are dealing with empty nest syndrome. How they manage this isolation as they seek to build new lives and new romances is critical to their health.

There are many ways to address mental health challenges. Doctors can prescribe medications, and other resources can be tapped, from mental health therapists to phone hotlines to church counseling to support groups. But in clawing back to a "good place" mentally, widows may do best when they have social circles they trust and can confide in. Dating and finding new romance can also help accelerate the pathway to good mental health. The added plus is that when widows do jettison themselves into the world of dating, the single and divorced people they meet can connect them to *their* social networks.

BROKEN HEART SYNDROME

It is not just what happens in a widow's head that is important. There are very real physical health challenges that go hand-in-hand with bereavement. Many widows are surprised when the death of a spouse wreaks havoc on their physical health.

Researchers have found mounting evidence that the first three months of bereavement are the roughest, health-wise. That's when loneliness most strongly correlates to physical illness and even early death. The latter is known as the Widowhood Effect, or what people used to quaintly call "dying of a broken heart." The health perils in widowhood can be direct—such as heart attacks or panic attacks—but they can also stem from erosion in good living and healthy habits.

"I managed to stay relatively healthy, but I drank more, stayed out later, ate fewer home-cooked meals," said Andrew, a young widower. "Whatever drugs I was doing at the time, I did more of those. But funny thing: I was a cigarette smoker—my wife was a chain smoker—and cigarettes were a regular part of our life. When my wife died, I immediately stopped smoking cigarettes."

Andrew said the restraint that came with being in a relationship, the tendency not to overdo it, evaporated right after his wife's death. "When you have someone in your life, you stay on a schedule, there's a certain routine, there's a certain level of prohibition," he said. "That all went away for a little while."

CAREGIVER RESENTMENT

There is another way in which health rears its head. Widows who served as caregivers for their dying spouses may be reluctant to take on that role again, instead of putting great value on the good health of potential new partners. On the dating scene, there is often an undercurrent that links attractiveness with health, especially among older daters who want to underscore their vitality and active lives. They work hard to avoid appearing frail. It is their defense.

Maura believed the widower she dated was unnerved by the thought of caring for someone again. His wife, whom he loved very much, had a long illness and he was dutifully at her side, but Maura said it was clear he did not want to do that again.

"I fall down and immediately he assumes it's something bigger," Maura said. "I think he's terrified about what happens to me. He's worried about having to take care of someone else. He is, consciously or unconsciously, projecting his thoughts about his wife onto me."

She said it wasn't just her physical health, but he was also on the lookout for memory lapses. "It scared the bejesus out of me. He was constantly saying things like, 'You lost your gloves. Last month you left the house without your wallet. You couldn't find your Fitbit charger,'" she said. "I talked to my doctor. I know I'm no more forgetful than anyone else." She no longer dates this man but they remain close friends. She surmised that he had focused on dementia and her health not only because of his caregiving past but because "he's afraid of being sick and on his own."

When Katie dated a widower, she sensed that he wanted someone at hand should his health fail. "He was afraid of needing someone to take care of him," she said. "He asked if I would stick with him through thick and thin."

A bicyclist, Katie was hit by a truck when she was in college and has lived with pain in the decades since, alleviating it as much as possible through Pilates, other exercises, and, more recently, medical marijuana. But she is aware that the aging process will be hard on her. Although her relationship with the widower ended for other reasons, she remembered the day she shared her health fears with him.

"I told him that someday I'm probably going to need a caregiver, too, so I can relate to his worries," she said. She encouraged him to take up new forms of exercise to help him get and stay healthy—and to get his energy level higher. "Depression makes you slower. Everything's slower," Katie said. "He was tired. He didn't sleep well. Meanwhile, I was on hyper-speed. Love-based emotions get you energized. I felt excited all the time."

Gretchen described herself as "extremely healthy," even during the period where she cared for her dying husband, who had a lengthy illness that depleted much of the couple's financial resources. Gretchen takes no medication and never has.

"My husband and I had a long marriage and a happy marriage," she said. "It was good until he became ill, and that's when the roles changed. You are now the caretaker, not the lover and wife." Her new partner is generally healthy, and he and Gretchen are active—walking, biking, kayaking—but she is relieved that he is well-insured.

"He has much better health insurance than I do. He has much better hospitalization coverage. He has assisted-living insurance," she said. "We have talked about what we would do if something happens to him."

These are probably not the conversations that twenty-somethings are having with their new romantic partners. But people who have served as caregivers have a reason to put great value on the health of any potential new partner—and to seek assurance as to what will happen if their health fails them.

When Susanna started dating after her husband's death, she steered away from men who were smokers and drinkers. Her boyfriend is five years younger than her, and they are both fit and focused on healthy living. "I exercise all the time, and I'm social," she said. Nonetheless, Susanna and her partner, whose father had Alzheimer's disease for twenty years before he died, have discussed health at length.

"We've agreed, if he gets to the point that he needs care, we'll put him somewhere that provides that care. I will not do full-time caregiving—and I don't expect him to," she said. "I know that one day I might have to go into a facility, into assisted living. I know that it will cost a lot. I know I have to make sure there is money to cover it."

Of course, "Who will care for me?" is not a concern limited to widows (and widowers). Relatively few Americans have insurance for long-term care, the ability or eagerness to move in with adult children or other family members, or the desire to live in a senior care facility—none of which are adequate substitutes for a caring partner. Most Americans wonder who will watch their back if they become ill or infirm.

Interestingly, while many widows find themselves in poor health after a spouse dies, there is also a segment who enjoy *better* health in widowhood.

"I am a compulsive overeater and about a year after my husband's passing, I started to focus on my health. I lost about a hundred pounds," said one widow with children still at home. "I did this for myself and for my children. My son was young and he worried I would die next. I have a whole life ahead to enjoy with my children. I did not intend to leave them with two dead parents."

Meg, meanwhile, said she "almost overreacted" on the health front after her husband's death. "I hired a personal trainer. I worked out a lot. I did triathlons."

Amy also committed to becoming fit after her husband died of a heart condition just shy of her seventy-third birthday. "When my husband died, I weighed a hundred and ninety-five pounds. I now weigh about a hundred and twenty-five. The way his death affected my health is that it made me think about eating properly and taking care of myself." Amy joined water aerobics and fitness classes. Once she started dating again, she encouraged the men she met to join her in stay-fit activities.

TALKING ABOUT HEALTH

It can be hard to muster the courage to discuss health with a potential new partner, especially if the discussion includes preexisting conditions. One of the authors of this book dreaded telling her new beau, a widower, about her history with cancer. His wife had died of cancer and she feared he might bolt. To his credit, he was unfazed. Nonetheless, it's harsh to judge someone who nursed a spouse through a life-wrecking illness and now hesitates, or even balks, at merrily linking up with someone who might promise them a rerun.

Just how to launch the health discussion—the etiquette for disease revelations, as it were—is the subject of websites, newspaper help columns, online blogs, and other resources. Oddly, the third date seems to be the consensus on *when* to raise the issue or, for really big secrets, once a widow is sure she wants a long-term relationship. These self-help sites encourage a widow to practice in advance what she will say, with the idea that this will go in the annals of her relationship as a quotable moment.

Clearly there are legal obligations behind some revelations. HIV and STDs immediately come to mind. Ailments such as bipolar disorder or other mental health challenges are part of a person's makeup and something their partner deserves to know. And, frankly, some medical histories or conditions are just too damn hard to hide.

Serious health conditions can undermine widows seeking companionship again. Take the widow with Stage Four cancer—or the ones with multiple sclerosis, heart conditions, mental illness, or any number of autoimmune illnesses. Most men or women on dating sites skip over profiles of people living with grave illnesses. Does a widow dare to hide her health woes? Does she lie when a potential date asks why she walks slowly or with a slight limp? Does she gloss over why she has so many doctor appointments or takes a menagerie of pills?

When writing her profile, does a widow with health challenges mention her illness, or does she wait to spring the news after a couple of dates? How long can she hide wicked surgical scars?

Great romance grows from unexpected places and, in an ideal world, everyone would be understanding. Practically speaking, however, we do not live in an ideal world. People we interviewed spoke of turning down a date with someone using a wheelchair or skipping over online profiles that hinted at illness. The months and years of caring for a dying spouse have left them wary of a repeat.

Dating apps for people with health challenges are slowly starting to emerge. These sites are most likely to connect people with an illness to someone else with an illness. Gutsy.dating, for example, is a UK-based dating app for people with celiac disease, Crohn's disease, irritable bowel syndrome, and other digestive health problems. Nolongerlonely.com is for people with mental illness. It is the early days for these types of apps so the verdict is still out on how well they work.

Widows can control their health and the health of any new significant other only so much. Relationships are a gamble. No matter how healthy someone is, their health can suddenly fail, especially in the later years. People fall for each other, there is chemistry, and sometimes perfect health is simply not part of the equation. The healthiest approach—no pun intended—is for widows to view medical challenges as they would any of the other quirks in a relationship. They are among the crazy elements that add interest, test commitment, and deepen love connections.

FROM MARTI'S BLOG

My Husband's Death Literally Broke My Heart

When 2014 started, I was convinced that this year would be better than the last three. I had a nice New Year's Eve and a more positive, overall feeling about my life moving forward without Tom.

Then the other shoe dropped.

March 4 that year was the fifty-year anniversary of my diagnosis with Type 1 diabetes. This motivated me in February to see a cardiologist just to make sure my heart was healthy. Long-duration Type 1s are at a much higher risk for heart disease, and sometimes while vigorously exercising, I had what might be construed as chest tightness. The situation worried me a little.

Despite being in shape, thin, energetic, and a healthy eater all my life, I agreed to a stress echocardiogram test one morning before work. It shockingly revealed an abnormality in my heart wall, which led to an angiogram the following week. This is where they thread a string-like device through a vein in the wrist to get pictures of the heart. I was scared shitless about this test, but I didn't think they would find anything too serious.

Imagine my horror at hearing the doctor say, while I was still in twilight sleep from the test, that my five major arteries were more than 90 percent blocked, and I needed multiple bypass heart surgery—pronto. The cardiac surgeon who visited me after the procedure said I was "a ticking time bomb."

I was ready to lose it. Through no fault of my own, I faced a much-needed procedure whereby they crack open the breastbone, remove the heart, insert into the heart new veins that they cut out of the left leg and sew the chest up with a whopping seven-inch incision. Oh yeah, and they insert tubes and wires in the chest that later get yanked out leaving crater-like scars.

I flipped out mentally and felt I'd rather die than go through this hellish surgery. I told my kids this and they got upset. Of course, at the time, I was angry, scared, and venting. And just two years earlier, their dad had died.

I waited four miserable days for the surgery, staying on a mattress with my daughter in my sister's basement. My sister lives near the hospital, and I felt safer there since I was now having chest pains and fretting that at any moment I would have a heart attack. My daughter and I were scheduled to visit my in-laws in Florida for her spring break and my vacation from a brutal Michigan winter. In fact, our plane was leaving the day I ended up having the surgery. From then on, we referred to my eight hellish days in the hospital as Spring Break 2014.

After the surgery, I had a few complications—due to hospital error—that kept me in the hospital three days longer. My daughter went back to college, but my son and sister were nearby. It was all really hard and, looking back, I'm not sure how I got through it. (I like to think Tom and my deceased parents were keeping an eye on me.)

I didn't have a perfect body, but it wasn't bad, and I rather liked it. After the surgery, my body looked butchered, but my spirits took an even bigger hit. Depression is common after bypass surgery. I wasn't so much depressed as in shock and angry that this happened on what felt like the heels of Tom's death. Even with Tom taking care of me, this surgery would have been awful, but without him, it was worse.

Still, I was blessed that my only sibling, my terrific kids, and my wonderful friends took turns staying with me, cooking for me, maintaining my house, helping me with just about everything during my first few weeks recuperating at home. It was the most helpless I have ever been.

So go figure. As I write this, I'm heading toward Week Six after surgery and looking at a couple more months of recovery and rehab. My mobility is limited. My chest hurts like hell. My leg, where they took out a vein that ran from my ankle to my groin, throbs, especially at night. This ordeal has aged me. But I'm alive and am told I will completely mend with time.

One of my dearest friends pointed out that I was lucky they discovered this. She is right. I could have ended up like my dear dad, dead in our living room at fifty-one from a massive heart attack.

· *10* ·

For Richer or Poorer

Everyone wants to ride with you in the limo, but what you want is someone who will take the bus with you when the limo breaks down.

—Oprah Winfrey

People in new relationships are willing to exchange gifts, bodily fluids, popcorn at the movies, HIV test results, and deep secrets. But will they share their FICO score?

Money. That old saying about it destroying relationships is not just a saying. Study after study has found that different approaches to finances, as well as divergent financial literacy levels, can wreak havoc on a romance. A 2015 Harris Poll commissioned by SunTrust Bank concluded that 35 percent of people in a couple cite finances as their greatest source of stress.[1]

Being in sync on money strengthens relationships. Yet research shows that most people wait more than three months into a dating relationship before they bring up finances, *if they discuss them at all*. Many of the people interviewed for this book did not know how much money their new partners earned, saved, or spent. Apparently, nobody wants to get naked when it comes to money.

Finances can be a stumbling block in any relationship, but there are additional considerations for widows. That's because when a woman loses a partner to death, she almost certainly faces a new financial reality. Widows may be left on a more precarious financial footing. A deceased spouse might have been the household breadwinner or, if not, at least a contributor to the joint economy. Benefits may be lost, such

103

as employer-paid health insurance or a retired spouse's social security income. If the death was preceded by an illness, medical bills may have gouged the bank account. And what about the post-retirement future the couple might have envisioned together? Is anything close to that even possible for the spouse left behind?

Gretchen's husband had a successful career and the couple was accustomed to regular vacations, a healthy 401K balance, and the other trappings of a comfortable life. Then he fell ill and Gretchen, who also worked, had to cut her hours at her job to help with his care.

"When he became ill, his income went to practically nothing, and I was only working thirty hours a week. Our finances went down the drain," she said. "Then when he died, I had medical bills to pay." Early in her widowhood, Gretchen was forced to sell the couple's home because her income was too scant to carry the mortgage.

She now is in a relationship with a wealthy man, but they don't commingle finances, and the house they share is in her name. She pays the mortgage, and he bankrolls the home improvements they make. (Separately, he has a house and a condo in his name. His son lives in one of them.) Gretchen covers her personal expenses.

"We keep the money separate," she explained. "I'm not looking at this relationship for greater financial security."

As a couple, they discussed selling her house and buying a home together in Florida. "I'm hesitant. What if something happens to one of us? What if something happens to the relationship?" she asked. The personal finance plummet that followed her husband's death has left her gun-shy about money.

For many women facing financial fragility, remarriage can be a concern because it makes a widow legally bound to pick up the tab for yet another life partner.

On the flip side, an insurance policy, pension, or survivor benefit might bring ready cash into the hands of a surviving spouse. That is well and good—as long as she is prepared to manage the windfall alone.

"My husband had a good job and we had life insurance. He died so quickly that we didn't run up exorbitant medical bills," said Meg. "But I had counted on his business knowledge—and suddenly I had this money to deal with." She said two friends, one an accountant and the other a financial planner, sat down with her and helped create a budget. "I was talking about going on an *Eat Pray Love* tour, and they weighed in with a firm 'No!' and 'Hell, no!'

"They allocated the money I needed to live, and suddenly I was a single person with a single income," she said. "But I could stay where I was living. They were really good about helping make sure of that." Even more, the friendly professional advice allowed her to eventually return to college for an MBA degree.

In a marriage, money habits grow as the relationship does and as life circumstances recalibrate. The extent of insurance coverage, promptness about paying bills, the size of an emergency stash (if there is one), cash management, and credit card use all determine whether a person is financially vulnerable, both now and in the future.

Susanna and her husband had an estate plan with all the details laid out. Their relationship was a second marriage for each of them and, during the eighteen years they had together before his death, they fine-tuned a formula that met their needs and goals. "Basically, our money was separate except when we made a big purchase together, then we paid proportionately," she said. "We had everything worked out, so we thought we'd be fine."

Within three months of his retirement, her husband was diagnosed with leukemia. She still worked. Suddenly their roles shifted, and she assumed more of the financial duties.

"I'd always done my own taxes. Now we did our taxes jointly and I took care of it," she said. "My husband had full insurance. As time went on, he qualified for Medicare. Then we bought supplemental insurance."

Although Susanna is financially stable, she saw how illness could make a surviving spouse fiscally vulnerable, and she has taken steps to make sure that does not happen with her current relationship. "If you marry somebody, if that person gets ill or sick or needs care, you have to spend down 50 percent of what you have before you can get any assistance for them," she said. "I have enough saved to be able to take care of myself for the rest of my life and that's where I'm staying.

"Even if I found somebody who was totally rich and they were going to leave it all to me, I feel that I could not afford to get married," she said.

ATTITUDES ABOUT MONEY

Spending isn't a problem for financially secure people. But overspending and compulsive spending are. Studies show that if one of the partners in a relationship feels that the other spends foolishly, the "marriage happiness" quotient is lower. Indeed, only extramarital affairs and alcohol abuse are bigger predictors than money of a relationship's demise.

In re-partnering, habits and priorities may need to be reshaped. And this can be challenging for both sides of the romance, especially if deep money-matter differences emerge—which they often do. Those diverging issues run the range from gambling (including lotteries) to spending on luxury cars and the latest electronic gadgets. Is the widow used to taking posh vacations? What about the new romantic partner? Does he (or she) seem overly generous with everyone? How do the money-management practices of the pair dovetail? Is the new boyfriend scraping to pay off his mortgage while the widow, also carrying a mortgage, wants to buy a bigger boat?

These differing views around money often surface as early as the first date, where the critical question may be "Who pays?"

Maura, for example, dated a widower who "has a lot of money," and he always picked up the check when they went out together. "When I was younger, starting when I was in college, I always paid my half of everything with the men I dated," Maura said. "Then I woke up. They all have more money than me. So if they pay when we're together, it's a small step toward equity."

"It's also a bit of a test of character and generosity," she said, adding that she would cover the bill for a friend of hers who was much less capable of paying than she was.

The "who pays" quandary isn't just for widows. Everyone seeking romance must sort through it. In fact, it has become a hot topic even among female millennials. They want to be courted and, although sympathetic about the cost of dating, they are disappointed when the old-fashioned "the man pays" chivalry is missing. A 2018 "Singles in America" survey by Match.com found that 91 percent of women think the man should insist on paying on the first date.[2]

There is an argument, however, that yesteryear chivalry is condescending. What if the woman makes more than the person she is dating? These split-the-bill conversations can be uncomfortable. And there's nothing more awkward than a showdown when the check arrives or, worse, a prolonged math exercise as two people attempt to figure out how much each owes (tip included).

Talking about money provides both sides an equal voice in laying out the terms of a relationship. However, some widows don't know how to approach the topic, in part because they feel unsure about the ways courtship rules shifted in the years they were away from dating. A couple on a date or a vacation can split the bill. The person who issued the invitation can pay. In a restaurant, one person can catch the bill and the other can cover the tip, then reverse the process the next time out. If there is a great disparity between the income levels of the two people, they can work out a compromise. Maybe, if both people agree to it, the one who has the most money always pays.

In other words, people are free to set up their financial collaboration in the way they feel is right and fair. "Who pays?" is not the critical question. It simply underscores the greater issue of the type of financial interweaving a couple opts to have.

Money conversations early in a relationship have the added benefit that they can unveil important information about people's values vis-a-vis money. Habits and attitudes peep out as early as the first date (which, inevitably, is the most important date). Do they under-tip or over-tip? Do they want every outing to be lavish or are economical at-home movie nights OK? Are multiple credit cards flashed with abandon or, conversely, are cheapskate tendencies on display? Does one person talk about money all the time, the other never? If new romantic partners are on different sides of these issues, is a budding relationship doomed?

FULL DISCLOSURE

Financial advisers claim that being financial opposites isn't necessarily a deal-breaker. The key to a healthy relationship is to talk—and adapt. Maybe it's not that the romantic partner carries major credit card debt but, rather, that he or she isn't doing anything about it. And when money is a problem for one of the new partners, it's important to look at what caused the shortfall. Was it illness, the recession, COVID-19, or an unexpected job loss?

Andrew was married for many years when his wife died in an accident. That's when he discovered that she had dropped the ball on some accounting duties in her care. At age thirty-six, he was suddenly scrambling to get back on a healthy financial footing.

"I found out after she died that there had been some stuff, like taxes, that she hadn't taken care of so I had to deal with that right away," he said. "There was the funeral to pay for. Since we were a two-income household, there was the loss of a paycheck, and I really felt that. And there were some medical bills I had to pay."

A widow with children still at home also suffered a financial about-face. "My children were sixteen, fifteen, and seven. I had suddenly become a single mom without an income," she said. "I signed up right away for Social Security . . . and my parents and in-laws were very generous. A fund was set up for our family." Four years into widowhood, her financial situation remains a struggle.

Almost universally, men and women bring different perspectives to the arena of personal finance. Women traditionally have shorter careers (taking time off to raise children or provide care for elderly parents and in-laws) and make less money during their working lives. Since they generally live longer, they must stretch their savings and investments over a longer retirement than men. For them, money can represent stability and security. That makes the lack of it a greater source of stress.

Additionally, financial literacy studies show that, for many reasons, women around the world share one thing: They have less financial knowledge than men.[3] Men, meanwhile, have more confidence about money and are willing to take greater risks. This doesn't necessarily mean they do a better job of managing their finances. But they think they do. Men are also more averse to seeking outside guidance, something that most experts say is critical to a strong financial portfolio. Still reeling from a partner's death, a widow may find herself facing a portfolio she doesn't understand and with no financial adviser to consult.

As to the question about sharing FICO scores: Do widows even *know* their FICO scores?

WHEN THE ROMANCE DEEPENS

Committed couples need shared ownership in their future, including their financial future. That said, while it's grand to commingle a lot of things, money isn't always one of them. For example, many financial counselors warn that the debt a widow brings to a romance should remain her debt alone. Even if she decides to marry, she should think hard—perhaps with outside financial advice—whether it is wise for both people in the relationship to combine everything. Sure, it can be great to help a struggling sweetheart to reduce his (or her) loans, but caution should be used when taking official responsibility for another person's debt.

Studies show that consumer debt is an equal-opportunity destroyer of relationships, regardless of whether couples are rich or poor, working class or upper-crust. If they accrue substantial debt, it strains their marriage, according to the National Marriage Project, a research project at the University of Virginia.[4] Interestingly, a separate study found that credit card debt increases the likelihood that a couple will spar over money. But it goes even further. Credit card debt is also a predictor of a couple fighting over *nonmoney* issues and of spending less and less time together.[5]

Widows need to be mindful that if pillow talk in a new romance turns to a conversation about marriage, every asset either person acquires after tying the knot could be held jointly. If widows are not on the same page as their new romantic partners when it comes to debt, retirement savings, investments, and other assets, they could be building relationships atop unsteady platforms. Among other things, widows should consider prenups, a notion that may seem foreign to them after commingling money in a marriage for many years.

Some people mistakenly view prenups as divorce contracts when they are more of an insurance policy designed to protect both members in a new relationship. Beyond love, a new relationship creates legal and financial connections, and a prenup—especially when there are children—is an acknowledgment of that. A prenup is no longer a document designed to protect the person with the most money in a relationship. It can also be shaped to address the needs of the most vulnerable member of this new partnership or to help define shared goals.

Prenup discussions should come early in relationships that are starting to feel serious.

THE FAMILY

With the death of a spouse comes the end of a familiar financial routine. Once a happy connection launches a new romance, the process must start again—or, at least, a decision must be made about how, and how much, financial sharing takes place. Often a widow does not only need to consider her financial security and wishes, but she has to take into consideration how money will affect family relationships.

When people enter new romances, they don't necessarily commit only to their new love interest. Often they commit to the whole tribe. Adult children, whether they express it or not, usually have expectations about inheritance. Children and stepchildren can emerge as natural competitors. That is why a widow and her new partner need to make new wills once they merge their lives. Those wills should detail who receives what.

How does a widow feel about giving or loaning money to adult children, either her own or those of her new partner? What about the house acquired by a widow and her deceased spouse? Will the new partner live there? Will they have any financial involvement in it? If so, will that disrupt the family's line of inheritance? Many widows describe their children's concerns about an inheritance or whether a new romantic partner might be a gold digger as one of the biggest reasons they choose to remain alone. That's unfortunate. Moving through life in a partnership, including a financial partnership, can make things easier and safer. It's just necessary to be smart about it—and there is a whole field of professionals, including accountants, financial advisers, and estate lawyers, who can help smooth the sharp edges in money discussions.

If the partners in a new couple are not 100 percent in line with one another's thinking about money, they'll need to identify how and where to compromise. They'll need to set rules and limits and delineate shared goals—and how to achieve them. They might follow a budget together, although always aware that having shared aims as a couple doesn't preclude each from holding individual financial goals. Some finance gurus advocate having separate yours, mine, and ours pots of money, claiming that if each member of the partnership has discretionary income, there is less feeling of an imposed restraint.

Any widow left holding the bag when a spouse dies understands too well the downside to letting one member of the couple play the primary role in managing finances. A new relationship offers a chance to redress this past mistake by making sure both romantic partners are involved in decisions about big purchases, *even if one person makes a whole lot more money than the other.* Aligning a person's say on finances to the size of their income is a trap. It opens the way for one person in the relationship to alone direct the couple's financial destiny.

They say that opposites attract. If one member of the couple is a saver and the other is a spender, there may be things they can learn from one another to end up in a stronger position together. There are many places to turn for guidance, including financial literacy classes, finance websites, online retirement calculators, personal accountants, library resources, and financial advisers.

Widows should also note that money management is not always marked merely by habit. Sometimes money is a stand-in for something else: power, self-esteem, control, independence, security. For example, if a person stiffs on a tip, are they cheap? Or are they saying something about their attitude toward working-class people? In other words, are they revealing a value? Such behavior could foreshadow how generous they will be as the new relationship proceeds.

Transparency about finances can be a bellwether for transparency in general. If a partner lies about money—hiding bank accounts, credit cards, or debt—what else do they lie about? Honest talk about finances can contribute to overall trust.

As life changes, so do goals, financial circumstances, and priorities. A widow and a new life partner should want to keep things relevant in their money plan. To make a go of it as a couple, it is imperative that they talk sooner, rather than later, and understand that money is easily interwoven with emotional issues. People who commit to a romantic partnership need to also invest in their mutual financial future.

Much in a romance is intangible: feelings, emotions. Money is the solid, concrete element. It should be honored and respected. Not only is it often true that two can live more cheaply than one, but a couple working in tandem may find ways to generate even *more* money to protect their tomorrow.

FROM MARTI'S BLOG

Ladies, It's OK to Put Away Your Wallet

The first time you meet a prospective date, you deal with who pays for the coffee, beer, glass of wine. I always offer to pay and more often than not am told to put away my wallet. Most men pay. That is the way it is.

The few men who wanted to split it down the middle or offered no money left me cold. It truly is an indicator of future money transactions and says a lot about a person's character.

When I am dating someone, I sometimes offer to pay and my offer is accepted. It is common courtesy to pick up the tab now and then. I took a guy out to dinner at an upscale restaurant. The bill? Roughly $100. He had picked up the tab many times so I felt good about paying. That particular time, he also insisted on paying the tip.

Most of the men I've gone out with pay whether it is for a meal, a movie, a play, or recreational sports such as kayaking or hiking at a park. When men present their credit card faster than I do, I typically let them handle the transaction. It is a good feeling, one that makes me feel like I am with a generous person who respects me. I know it sounds old school, but it is an old school I appreciate.

Once you start dating someone for any length of time, it is good to have a conversation about who pays for what. Talking about any topic makes things more comfortable. Money and spending is an especially important topic to address openly.

• *11* •

Merging Lives

*All the wealth in the world cannot be compared with the happiness
of living together, happily united.*

—Marie-Marguerite d'Youville, widow, nun, and saint

*O*ne of the most fascinating things about talking to widows who have
entered new relationships is the dynamic way they are reimagining the
practicalities of romantic life. A generation ago, widows were more
likely to remarry and replicate what they had just lost or, alternatively,
to disavow love forever. But widows today, especially the baby boomers,
are rewriting the way two lives can come together in love.

For starters, many widows in the generation that shacked up together in college have orbited back to that option, building late-in-life
romantic relationships without the benefit of marriage. Even when they
do choose nuptials, some widows are bypassing traditional vows. No
more "for richer or poorer" or "in sickness and in health." They're
keeping their finances separate, signing prenups, and even asking partners
to produce proof of long-term care contracts in the event of future illness. Still, others are taking more nonconventional paths, living together
certain days of the week or marrying but residing in separate homes.

Widows are shaping partnerships the way they want largely because
society no longer cares very much whether people follow the traditional
rules.

If new romantic partners are drawn to each other like moths to
a flame (ah, the dangers of love) and spending enough nights of the
week together that their bills are neglected, their laundry is piling up,
their odometers are working double-time, then they're thinking about

the next step. (The isolation caused by COVID-19 added even more urgency for some couples. Not making a decision during the pandemic meant a long stretch in physical isolation, something many want to avoid in the future.)

So what do they do? Move in together? Marry? Marry and live apart? (Yes, that is a real thing.) Friends and family may also be hovering along the sidelines, offering perhaps not-so-helpful advice. Some people in a widow's circle may be happy, even relieved, to see that she is re-partnering. But there are others, because they care, who worry.

COHABITING

They fell in love amid the tropical heat of Miami. He is a widower whose wife died after a long illness. She is a divorcee. Their courtship flourished through a mutual love of travel, boating, and socializing with friends. They roamed around the world together. They visited one another's adult children, celebrating their forward steps in life. After an extended time together, they announced their engagement. But this couple has no intention of marrying. They live together and their engagement, now many years old, was simply their way of making a public commitment to one another.

Cohabitation, once seen as the option of young people or those who are not fully committed to one another, is rising in popularity among older couples. In fact, the Pew Research Center's analysis of US Census data for 2016 found that the jump in the number of unmarried Americans living together had been driven by *older couples*.[1] Some eighteen million couples live together without marriage in the United States, the research found, and four million of them—nearly 23 percent of the total—are age fifty and older. That means the number of older "cohabiters" had leaped nearly 75 percent over a decade.

Susanna, a widow, is happily involved with a man who has been divorced for a long time. They have been together as a couple for several years, but she never wants to remarry. She described their formal status as "living together," but there's a footnote. It depends on the day of the week. Their cohabitation begins every Thursday and ends every Monday morning when Susanna heads off to work and her retired partner retreats to a house he owns an hour away.

"It makes life a little simpler," Susanna explained. "At some point we might buy a house together, but that's not written in stone—and I don't want it written in stone."

Why do some widows forgo marriage? Living together can be a great thing. It offers couples wider social circles, sex, and sometimes—although not always—more financial stability. In some ways, it also provides preemptive protections missing from marriage. A widow can't be held responsible for her live-in lover's credit card debt, for example, and her partner's assets won't be counted if she seeks to qualify for Medicaid. A large national study found that distinct from marriage, older people living together are also less likely to take on long-term caregiving duties if a partner becomes ill.[2]

In other words, it is not the fear of commitment that prompts widows to forgo remarriage. More often it has to do with practicalities. Sometimes there are tax disincentives or disruptions to pension or military benefits if a woman remarries. A widow may take a more prudent approach to finances than her new partner; living together rather than marrying allows her to protect her savings, her credit card score, and her debt-free reputation. Although some families are shocked or uncomfortable when a widowed matriarch chooses cohabitation over marriage, the living together option often helps calm offspring worried about their inheritance or the fate of family heirlooms.

Some widows did not have happy marriages. They are wary of being locked into that situation again. Cohabitation offers an option that is less absolute, allowing them to see what real love might entail without the fear of a forever commitment.

Widows who want a life together with their new partners but don't want the legality of marriage sometimes opt for a runaround solution: a spiritual ceremony. They may bring together family and friends to exchange vows but in a way that does not bind them—formally, legally, or economically—under the law. Although not a legal wedding, the ceremony allows the couple to publicly express their dedication to one another. They may see this solution as a sweet spot that lets them underscore their devotion to each other while still protecting their independence.

Tax, investment, and legal experts can provide laundry lists of how widows should protect themselves when choosing to cohabitate. What if the widow moves into her new partner's home and, after years together, he has to move to a care facility for some reason? Will his children or heirs boot her out of the house? What if the widow or her mate becomes ill and needs assistance with day-to-day living? What guarantees are there that they will help one another? Lawyers say a cohabitation agreement can provide the legal protections needed.

For younger widows with children headed to college, there may be one big benefit to living together rather than tying the knot: marriage could affect their children's eligibility for financial aid. The Free Application for Federal Student Aid (FAFSA) looks at the income and assets of both spouses in a marriage, regardless of whether the stepparent is contributing to college expenses.[3]

FIRST COMES LOVE, THEN COMES MARRIAGE

The growing trend toward cohabitation does not mean marriage has headed the way of rotary phones and paper road maps. Marriage is still the most common destination for widowhood romance.

For some widows, cohabitation is merely a stepping stone on a long journey toward marriage. Others may take a more direct path to the altar. They crave the intensity and security that come with wedding vows. They want to make a legal declaration of their commitment, to follow the conventional script. If they were happily married before, they still believe firmly in the institution of matrimony. They envision beautiful, merged families and joyful new lives—and relish the prospect of aging together.

"We're in this forever. This is a lifetime commitment," said Louise, who reconnected with a long-ago boyfriend after her husband's death. "I had a good relationship with my husband, but I feel like this is a soul match." She and her new partner haven't talked about marriage yet, but she's certain they will—and that is what she wants.

Widows remarry for love, companionship, sex, or even security (financial and otherwise). They may be gun-shy about relationships that are not defined as permanently entrenched. They may fear being left alone and, as a result, crave legal protections for themselves and their new partners. After all, a widow has already felt the deep devastation that comes from the loss of a partner.

Marriage also carries practical benefits. There may be more tax breaks for a married couple than one that is cohabitating. (For the very wealthy, marriage can be a safety shield against inheritance taxes.) A spouse is entitled to take leave from work to care for a family member, but the partner in a live-in relationship may not be. Likewise, spouses can make medical decisions for one another. Imagine being a widow in an unmarried relationship where a partner becomes gravely ill—before designating a medical representative—and watching his children make all the decisions about his care and future, including who can even be at his bedside.

Statistically, widowers are more likely than widows to remarry. That was the case with Katie's last romantic partner, whose wife had died several years earlier. "He was on super-speed about moving the relationship forward. He proposed to me. He wanted to get married our first summer," said Katie, who is divorced. "He was happy in his marriage, and he wanted to be happy again."

For Katie, however, remarriage would be financially punitive given the terms of her divorce, and she was unsure about making that sacrifice, even though she felt at the time that she may have finally found her soul mate. She also feared that things were moving too fast. "Sometimes I wondered that because he lost his wife, he worried about losing me."

The relationship did not endure, but before it fell apart, the couple lived together—or, as she put it, "he had his own closet, he had his own bathroom" in her home for a time—and they contacted a real estate agent with an idea of buying a house together. They also traveled to Latin America to scope out possible retirement destinations, even though she felt tethered to her friends and had hoped he would consider putting down roots where she lived.

Another woman said she assumed the widower she dated would want to marry. That was also the future she envisioned. She surmised that he was anxious to return to the situation he had before, one that made him happy. In preparation, she pared down her belongings and indicated her willingness to move. But the talk of marriage did not gain much traction and the relationship evaporated after a few years.

On the flip side, some widows quickly throw themselves into new marriages only to find that they don't last. They want to recapture love, to re-create the happy life they had before, and that's all admirable. But sometimes it takes more than aspirations.

WHERE WILL I PUT MY STUFF?

Whether through marriage or cohabitation, the idea of moving in to-gether can feel gleeful. The work in executing it can feel overwhelming.

What about children? Whose house or apartment becomes the new home? Does the couple have to find "neutral" territory that has no con-nection to either of their previous lives? And how will other anchors in their lives—jobs, friends, extended family—be affected by any decisions they make together?

Widows don't necessarily have to blend their finances with those of their new partners, but they do have to commingle (or reform) their habits. Older couples, especially, may find themselves working hard to dovetail two complex lives. And there's also the thorny issue of their belongings. In this society where downsizing and decluttering are a na-tional pastime, what happens to all the *stuff*?

Gretchen's romantic partner lives in her house "75 percent of the time." The rest of the time he's at his retreat in northern Michigan or a house he shares with his son. She readily admitted that "space is an issue" in her home and that is why this arrangement was created. She said it felt as if there was plenty of room in her house for two people until her significant other asked for a room of his own. "He needed space for his paperwork. I said, 'You have your other house,'" she recalled. "Frankly, if he didn't have that other house, I wouldn't have invited him to live with me. No thanks. I like my space."

Possessions can be tricky. We know a woman who set a condition for remarriage: her beau could not bring any of his furniture. Once they married and set up house together, she also told him he had to lose his magazine collection.

It's hard to part with material possessions. Sometimes it's even harder for widows because of the emotional connections. Today's off-spring are part of a generation that increasingly is rejecting the notion of taking on the family china or heirlooms, so there's no channel for passing cherished items along. At the same time, new love partners may not relish living with the trappings of a widow's previous marriage. At a nonprofit meeting hosted by a couple in their Washington, DC, home, lovely crystal wine glasses were set out for use. One guest hesitated, saying she worried about breaking a glass. The hostess cheerily replied: "Oh, don't worry. They belonged to his first wife."

Other practical considerations also come into play, including the cost of housing in urban areas. A widower carrying on a long-distance relationship for years lived alone in a small apartment in New York City's Bedford-Stuyvesant neighborhood. He loved his place and the neighborhood. It was convenient, interesting, and rent-controlled but, unfortunately, it wasn't big enough for two people. Once his girlfriend decided they should move the relationship up a notch and set up house-keeping together, things started heading downhill.

The girlfriend was willing to live in New York, but the couple could not afford another property, especially since she had left her job to be with her boyfriend. The idea of moving to New Jersey or north of New York to Westchester County meant a lifestyle change he balked at. The solution? They broke up. They wanted to live together but they couldn't figure out a way to make it work.

The merger of two households requires that the emotional power of widows' belongings—from previous wedding photos to love letters to family furniture—has to be neutralized. Luckily, that often can be as simple as putting them in a private area of the new shared digs or even in storage.

Alternatively, a couple that wants marriage but is daunted by the physical move and downsizing involved can opt for an in-between approach: married but living apart.

LIVING APART TOGETHER

More and more widows are giving serious thought to a hybrid commitment that merges the best of both worlds. They marry but maintain separate homes. The question "What do we do with our stuff?" becomes moot when there are separate houses. Simply put, everything stays where it has always been.

Marriage with separate abodes has become a movement with its own name: Living Apart Together. This phenomenon is gaining ground in Europe with spillover in the United States, and some researchers even see it as a historically new family form. These committed couples who live in separate residences may be across the country from one another, across the hall in the same apartment building, or in side-by-side housing units. (Long live the duplex.) They do not pick this option because jobs or family obligations force them to have separate addresses. They live apart by choice but with the same expectations of fidelity and commitment as in a traditional marriage.

English writer Mary Wollstonecraft, the mother of *Frankenstein* author Mary Shelley, and her husband, philosopher William Godwin, were early adopters of the Living Apart Together philosophy. They lived in adjoining houses—in 1797! Helena Bonham Carter and Tim Burton had adjoining houses during their thirteen years of marriage. Novelist Margaret Drabble and her husband, biographer Michael Holroyd, used to live in separate houses, although they eventually abandoned that for a shared space in London. Another author, Booker Prize winner Arundhati Roy, and her environmentalist husband Pradip Krishen, still maintain separate residences in India. And famously (or infamously), Woody Allen and Mia Farrow had separate apartments on opposite sides of Central Park during the twelve years they were in a romantic relationship.

Although not married, attorney and academic Anita Hill—best known for her testimony during Clarence Thomas's Supreme Court nomination—has been in a committed romantic relationship for many years. Throughout it, she and her partner have lived separately. A Chicago lawyer and a New York entertainment agency founder continue to live in their respective cities, even after marrying. Phone calls and emails keep them joined when they are not in the same city. During the times they are together, they said, every activity carries the energy of a first date.

Some widows jump on the Living Apart Together bandwagon because they like the independence that comes with a home of their own. They may want a place where they can have their friends and families gather without putting strain on their new relationship. They may even remember the uneven divisions of labor that marked their first marriage and decide to bypass that by living apart. A widow who remarries a man with health challenges may keep her household so she isn't pulled into the vortex of his daily caregiving.

Without question, it's a distinctive type of living arrangement. Widows who put this option on their wish list talk about the confusion it generates. When real estate agents find out a couple is in the market for adjacent houses or duplexes, they make the assumption it's to live in one and rent out the other. The finances of maintaining two households can be a deal-breaker for some couples. And there are logistical challenges with separate addresses, including who stays at which house on what nights. But there are also many pluses. The arrangement gives the couple the human connection they desire, but also the time apart and space they want. In other words, it gives them both companionship and autonomy. By maintaining separate residences, the ground rules are kept simple.

Separate addresses keep some people together, but they are not the answer for everyone. Living separately while married may put one member of the couple at greater risk of ending up in a care facility. Some people feel more vulnerable and unsupported without a partner close at hand. And living together while married is certainly more common and affordable. Still, Living Apart Together allows members of a lasting relationship to bypass the drama of which house to keep, how to retain independence, or how to fulfill a desire for solitude within a relationship.

YOURS, MINE, AND OURS

Married or cohabitating, some second-marriage couples tilt toward the idea of creating multigenerational homes. These are households where two or more adult generations live together—typically parents, adult children, and grandchildren—and they are on the rise. A 2018 Pew Research Center analysis of US Census data found that more than sixty-four million residents of the United States live with multiple generations under one roof.[4] That's one-fifth of the US population and growing. The Pew study found that multigenerational households were on the rise across nearly all racial groups and ages, although the prevalence was greatest among Asians, Hispanics, and immigrants.

Multigenerational homes are a solution to many problems, among them long-term care dilemmas and rising housing costs. For the multi-generational option to have a happy ending, a widow and her partner must search carefully for the space that matches their particular situation. Once they find it, ground rules are needed. Some housing experts even recommend putting together a "real estate prenup" or some other formal document that addresses things like household expenses and who pays them, what furniture gets moved and what doesn't, how household chores are divided, as well as an exit plan for when or if a household member moves out.

Multigenerational households may not be a good option for people who struggle with open communication and group decision making. Clearly it is not for everyone. But it is another choice for widows (even without mates) who want companionship and the security of a family-like environment while maintaining their freedom. It is awfully nice for a widow to have a family unit around her when she is not up to par to get groceries or pick up a prescription. Likewise, a widow who is a grandparent may help out with childcare. Cooking, yard work, and other household chores can be shared.

Regardless of what living situation widows choose, the relationships they envision may look very different from the ones they used to have. Some may embrace the same vows they took in their first marriages or slightly modified versions. They know what works best for them. Other widows, however, are thumbing their noses at cultural precepts about later-in-life romance. They are choosing to reenter relationships in new and even heretical ways, without marriage, in separate homes, with happy disregard to the concerns of friends and family, and with unusual solutions for managing finances and health challenges. One widow we interviewed was in a relationship with a married man. Another was in a polyamorous relationship—involved with a man who had an open commitment with his other partner.

How does each widow decide what's best for her?

No single answer fits everyone, but there are goals to aim for:

- A new (or customized) partnership that has both good balance and strong boundaries.
- A relationship where both members listen to each other and *show they are listening.*
- A dynamic that shows the couple knows how to respectfully argue, how to negotiate, and when to recognize whether the conflict is worth it. The ability to manage conflict may be the most powerful skill in a romance.
- The acknowledgment that while each member of the partnership has a past, the couple is looking forward together.
- Respect for what each person in the love match brings to a custom-built relationship, rather than what each leaves behind.
- New habits and routines. A new romance means new patterns, a fresh start. A widow is changed by grief and now is being

changed by new love. The dynamic may not look like anything she has known in the past.

Research by scholars at the University of Denver and the University of Louisville found that it's not how couples merge their lives—cohabitation, marriage, or some alternative—that matters so much as the way they reach that decision. More succinctly, it's the slide-versus-decide phenomenon.[5] "Decide" means people are thinking carefully about what they want in their romantic partners and their shared lives, including their sex lives and, for younger widows, the way they raise children together. It means keeping those aspirations in mind as they navigate relationships. By necessity, conscious decision making also means taking the time to communicate, a habit that spills over into mutual goal-making and troubleshooting on other important issues.

"Slide" is exactly what it sounds like: the place where people end up when inertia rules. Couples who decide rather than slide gain practice collaborating successfully. The partnering skills they intentionally forge lay the foundation for a happy relationship.

One way for a couple to usher along the conscious decision-making process is through a love audit. This involves thinking about the elements and patterns in their lives, separate and together, that bring happiness and then writing them down. A widow's list might say: *reading the Sunday papers together, spending quality time alone with my grandson, going to concerts with my friends, cooking meals together with my sweetheart.* A love audit also examines the issues that cause stress for each member of the couple separately and for their partnership. Among the examples a widow might cite are: *commuting to his place for dates on work nights, managing the chores and expenses of a big house alone, wishing he was with me on the days I need to talk with someone.* During this exercise, patterns emerge—more time together, less time together, more commitment, less independence—that help a widow understand where her romance is naturally directing itself. An online search of "relationship audit" turns up several websites with questions that help a couple assess how they're doing.

The way that two people go about formalizing a new relationship is always fascinating to watch. The widows we interviewed offered wide-ranging approaches to their lives with new romantic interests, while also acknowledging that merging lives is a bit like changing lanes. There's

some maneuvering and glancing back to make sure the lane is clear before shifting over, while hoping that a blind spot doesn't cause a crash.
The goal is to move the journey forward as smoothly as possible.

FROM MARTI'S BLOG

Fond Memories of Family House, but Daughter's Angst Challenging

After twenty-eight eventful years, I sold the family house and moved pre-
cisely two miles northeast to a smaller, more modest 1950s house.

It was quite the undertaking emotionally and physically.

It started in November 2017, on a rainy, cold day when I was bored. I
drove around my area looking for houses for sale. The listing service with my
agent was turning up no properties that fit my requirements: three beds, two
baths, small yard.

I went down a block I had never been on and saw a cute ranch with a for
sale sign. Hmmm, I wondered. Why did my agent not tell me about this one?
I found it on a real estate website and saw the potential. It hadn't come to our
attention because it has only two bedrooms. I called my agent and we got in the
next day.

The house needed a good deal of work and the furnishings, wall colors,
and carpet were all dated. But it showed promise and had many of the things I
was looking for. A few days later, I made a lower-ball offer that took into consideration the house had a leaking, decrepit roof, no AC, and a half-remodeled
bathroom. It was accepted.

I bought the house that month—signed the contract Thanksgiving morning
and immediately began hiring tradespeople to get the house into shape. Project
managing this house kept me busy for much of the winter. Meanwhile, I also
hired and managed workers to fix up our 1929 family house, which needed many
repairs and improvements to meet the city's rigorous inspection codes.

The process was pleasant until about March, when my grown daughter,
who I have a close and wonderful relationship with, started outwardly express-
ing her emotions about leaving our beautiful house brimming with leaded and
stained glass and original walnut moldings, and all its wonderful memories. I,
too, had emotions, but knew I had to get out before my daughter left me to join
her long-time boyfriend in another city. I did not want to live in that house with
all its memories alone again. After Tom's death, I did it for four years when my

daughter was away at school, but I was well then and working full time. My life was good. The stiff cancer diagnosis in 2016 and the resulting mobility shortcomings gave me a greater incentive to live in a smaller, one-story house.

The memories we had of life in the house as a family of four, then three, then two, then one, now two again were both sweet and sorrowful. Tom loved the house. If he were alive, it would have been nearly impossible to pry him out of there. Now my daughter was following in her father's footsteps, insisting that selling the house was a mistake. It was making the transition away from home even harder. I was glad I had no partner in my life to weigh in on all this drama with my daughter.

She became moody and angry. She was slow to pack her twenty-eight years of clothes, toys, photos, and countless bins of school memorabilia. I'd lay in bed at night in pain from cancer and stress about how I was going to move all the stuff in this house to another, smaller house. I'd fret about who was going to do all the moving because I could not lift a box weighing more than a pound. I would have to rely on friends, family and professional movers to do it all. I couldn't sleep. I lost my appetite.

As it turned out, the old house sold in one day to a young couple. More emotions. More questions. Did I sell it for too cheap? Should I have taken the first offer? Should I be buying a house that could accommodate more house guests or a permanent resident? More worry ensued about moving; more harsh words erupted with my daughter.

But the months and weeks went by and slowly things got packed up by my dear, strong, healthy friends and family members. My son and daughter-in-law helped by taking stuff that they wanted to their house. The new house slowly was remodeled; the handyman nearly took residence in the old house to get it in shape for its sale. I still laid sleepless most nights.

In late April, we moved to the new house. In May, I closed on the family house. It took friends and family again to help me unpack dozens of heavy boxes, organize stuff, sell things, and give away items mostly by leaving them on the curb.

We are nearly settled into the new house but, despite me hiring an inspector who said back in December that I had a good house, I am finding more and more undisclosed flaws.

My daughter will be leaving me soon and that's OK. The next challenge will be feeling alright about living in this ranch alone.

• 12 •

One Is (Not) the Loneliest Number

What a lovely surprise to finally discover how unlonely being alone can be.

—Actor Ellen Burstyn

Finding Love after Loss: A Relationship Roadmap for Widows is written for women willing to move beyond grief to seek romantic love again. Interestingly, in tracking the stories of widows, we found that some who set out to end the solitude of solo living after their partners' deaths ended up remaining alone—but this time often by choice rather than a result of tragedy.

No remarrying, no cohabitating. Maybe not even any serious connecting. A return to conventional relationships may not be the answer for all widows.

"While I have done some dating in the years since my husband died, I have also been quite surprised at how well I fit into the single life," said Meg, who became a widow at forty-five. "I never expected to be single in the first place, and I didn't expect to be single now, but I ended up getting it, and I genuinely enjoy it, much to the consternation of virtually everyone around me."

Every widow is shaping her own new story, and it takes time to discover the person she has become through sorrow. Although a widow may start with a different aspiration, the prospect of a new romantic relationship may start to feel like a less interesting path than solo-adventuring. After serious dating or even after finding romance, some women discover that they prefer the independence and privacy that comes with widowhood. They are relieved to be free of the responsibility of other people. Whether they choose casual dating, no-strings-attached sexual liaisons, or celibacy, they finally can pursue the ambitions that were bypassed by marriage.

Others take a more laissez-faire approach, accepting that new love may or may not be part of their future. They haven't shut the door, but while they wait to see what life hands them, they relish their singleness. Some widows lived in unhappy marriages. They, too, may have reasons for embracing single living with no attachments.

Two generations ago, most widows were too financially fragile to choose the single life. They would have remarried or lived with their children. Then the expansion of Social Security benefits, the feminist movement, and the reshaping of the American family slowly started to broaden the opportunities available to women. Women also entered the workforce in increasing numbers, forging a degree of financial independence. In more recent years, much of the stigma of being alone has dissipated in contemporary society and it is OK to travel, dine out, or go to social engagements alone.

Widows who remain single today are joining an unprecedented demographic. Being unpartnered is more common than ever, a rising trend across all age, race, and ethnic groups. About half the adults in the United States are single, compared with 22 percent in 1950, according to the Bureau of Labor Statistics. A Pew Research Center report in 2014 estimated that by the time today's young adults reach age fifty, about one in four of them will never have married.[1] Within that framework, about a third of the people who are not in committed relationships also live alone. (The others thrive in a continuum of living arrangements.)

Right after the death of a spouse, living alone can feel like a nightmare. Women find it scary to be on their own after years of couplehood, and many are overwhelmed being in the homes they once shared with partners who helped manage the upkeep and maintenance. Gradually some of these widows find ways to compensate for the emptiness. They move to smaller homes or to apartments and condos in active neighborhoods. They pick up skills that make them feel more competent and confident. They forge new friendships. Single living starts to feel like a good fit.

"I thought I'd be married by now. It has really surprised me that I haven't been. I was twenty-eight when I married and now I'm exploring if I'm OK being single," one widow told us. "After my husband died and I started to date, even when I met guys I really liked, I would be the one to back away.

"I have been opened up to a new life I didn't know was there," she said.

SOLITUDE AND HAPPINESS

Some women, after dating successfully online for a while, decide they don't need a new relationship to be happy. They may reject opportunities to begin committed relationships or rebuff offers of marriage. They may come to think of their foray into dating as a chance to help them consider *all* options—and they choose singlehood. A Canadian study found that 74 percent of senior-aged women in that country reported being highly satisfied living alone.[2]

Friends and family can turn out to represent the most powerful relationships, more satisfying than marriage. Widows who choose to remain single often have built new friendships—or fiercely maintained satisfying old ones—that they do not want to disrupt by simultaneously trying to juggle romantic entanglements. People who are single by choice are more likely than married people to stay in touch with friends, neighbors, parents, and siblings.[3] Although this phenomenon is more prominent for never-marrieds than widows and other singles who were previously married, it is clear that being single increases social connections.

One study asked twenty-three hundred people age sixty-two or older to name five people in whom they could confide. Single respondents came up with many more names than did married or cohabiting respondents.[4] The researchers concluded that people on their own get greater rewards from their friendships than do couples. Not surprisingly, people who live alone also invest more time and energy in their friendships.

Some widows believe they can live more authentic lives if they remain single. When people marry young, they tend to grow and change in tandem with a spouse, accommodating differences. People who approach relationships later in life are often more set in their habits and preferences. The prospect of dovetailing those into a new relationship may feel like too much work.

SINGLE BY DEFAULT?

While some widows consciously choose to live alone, others may find themselves on their own because they have not found suitable new partners. This may be permanent or it may be "for the time being." Some social scientists believe that single people today are more likely to hold out in hopes a perfect partner will appear.

A widow's choice to remain single might also grow from her fear of outliving another partner or, worse, being a caregiver again if a new partner becomes ill. (The thought of nursing another spouse through cancer or severe heart disease may be enough to keep a widow single through infinity.) In other cases, widows may feel certain there is no one out there who comes close to their deceased spouse, or they may cling to the idea that it would dishonor their marriage. Confident in their decision to go forward on their own, they find single living active and buoyant.

"I can't date. It feels disloyal," said Evie, whose husband was her childhood sweetheart. "I still feel married. That will never change for me. I can't even think about another relationship."

Widowhood is often wrapped up in mythologies about the broken-hearted spouse who is left behind after a fairy-tale married life. In truth, some marriages are not happy and women are relieved to be freed from them. One widow told us about the coldness and emotional distance in her marriage. Another said her husband had an affair after he found out he was dying, breaking their trust even as she was caring for him.

These women have no interest in returning to the type of commitment that kept them from joy.

"We didn't have a good or close marriage and when my husband died, I felt like I finally got my life back," said Jennifer, who was married for forty years and raised three children with her husband. "He was a perfectly nice guy, he wasn't mean-spirited or anything like that, but he had no interest in anything I cared about.

"I'm not interested in even dating," she said. "I'm an obsessed potter. I knit, I sew, I go to New York and visit museums or go to the theater. And I have wonderful friendships with women. That is what makes me happy."

ADDING ILLNESS TO WIDOWHOOD

Not all widows are older, but most are. And the older people become, the more likely they are to live with some type of disability, from mobility challenges or any number of autoimmune diseases. The US Census Bureau's American Community Survey in 2017 found that 35 percent of people age sixty-five and over reported some type of disability.[5] Of course, not all disabilities are equal and attitudes (and misconceptions) about what people with disabilities feel and want are as varied as the human species itself.

In a perfect world, a disability should not affect whether people can enter successful relationships—and many differently abled people do find lasting love. But the reality is that having a disability can make it more complicated to find a new partner, especially when caregiving may be part of the package. The unpredictability of some health challenges puts extra pressure on a relationship. Sometimes widows with disabilities are discouraged from seeking new partnerships because the journey feels too daunting.

On a practical level, the physical and emotional changes that come with treatments for a chronic illness can also affect dating and relationships. Potential mates may be unwilling to take on new partners with cancer or other serious illness. (Cancer.net, an online network for people with cancer, offers suggestions on how to approach dating during treatment.)[6] At the same time, some widows told us that managing health challenges while also trying to date was too overwhelming.

Remaining single is not without its complications. Interestingly, while many widows face family opposition once they start dating, others find that friends and families don't respect the decision *not* to date. Even widows who are secure and happy in that decision face pushback. Damned if you do and damned if you don't.

Good lives are rich with personal connections, from family links to friendships to romantic partnerships. They are what make people whole. But they are not all needed at every point in one's life. Some of the happiest people are single by choice.

FROM MARTI'S BLOG

Be Careful What You Share on Dating Sites

Recently while on an online dating site, I started up an email relationship with a self-employed defense attorney. While he was not especially attractive, he was smart and he was literate, which is important to me.

I was thinking maybe we should meet for coffee and was about to suggest it. But things can change in a minute, especially on a dating site, especially when you are honest.

Suddenly, this guy shared with me that he was a cancer survivor. He explained that cancer was found in a couple of his organs, and the disease was serious. But, not to worry, because he had miraculous care by an oncologist who cured him.

Well, I was, in a way, delighted to find this out because I have cancer. What a common bond we had.

At first, I had no intention of sharing my health history with anyone online. But when this guy spilled his cancer story, I immediately wrote him that I had Stage IV breast cancer. I explained that I had been treated and was doing well now.

Literally within two minutes, the guy hit me with an email that detailed the names of all his doctors, his hospital, treatment, etc. and said I should contact them. Then he coolly said "see ya." He added maybe we could just be friends and then virtually disappeared.

This was a new experience, but one that reinforced that you should not tell anyone online about something so personal.

Of course, in this case, the guy showed his true colors and saved me from ever having to meet someone so shallow.

· 13 ·

The Time of the Widow

It's never too late to start over!

—Lynne Gentry, author of *Reinventing Leona*

*W*idows are having a pop culture moment.

Once upon a time, widows in movies, theater, and TV were relegated to a limited number of roles. They were lustful schemers (Merry Widow), homicidal (Black Widow), old and frail, and, almost always, tragic. Rarely were they allowed new and multilayered lives after their spouses died. On the rare occasion, they were permitted to date or yearn for partners, although the best love interests available to them might not even be living. (In the 1940s movie and related 1960s TV series *The Ghost and Mrs. Muir*, for example, the widow fell in love with the ghost of a sea captain.)

More than anything, just as widows hovered in the shadows of our bigger society for generations, they were also mostly absent from the big screen and TV shows. If they happened to appear, it was rarely as the main characters.

Fast forward. The last several years, surprisingly, have brought a cascade of TV shows and movies that represent widows as three-dimensional characters with all the strengths and flaws of any other demographic group. Think Kate Beckinsale in the TV series *The Widow* (even though her widowhood was temporary); the widow buddy series *Dead to Me* about two women who meet in grief therapy; and the Facebook-produced show *Sorry for Your Loss*. There was also the Netflix series *Virgin River* following a young widow as she started a new life as a nurse practitioner in a small town in California and the British sitcom

133

Mum tracing a fifty-something widow and her family right after her husband's death.

It isn't just the small screen. Widows have surfaced in greater numbers in films. In the aptly named film *Widows*, four Chicago women plan a heist to repay a crime boss whose money was stolen by their now-deceased husbands. Helen Mirren's 2019 film *The Good Liar* followed a widow targeted by a romancing scam artist. A young widow with three children was the focus of the 2020 drama *The Secret: Dare to Dream*.

Literature has always been more expansive about widows, although many fictional widows seem both defined and challenged by what they no longer have—money, mates, and a place in conventional society. What has shifted about widows' stories in books in recent years is a growing interest not in fiction about widows but, rather, in memoirs written *by* widows. As famous baby boomers age, they are joining the growing list of people who have lost a life partner. Iconic women among them—actors, authors, activists—have taken to publishing their stories.

Why does any of this matter? The inclusion of widows in mass media is important because popular culture influences the way we see groups. It sends a message that widows, a demographic that often feels on the fringes, not only is ubiquitous but it merits attention. It also helps shape our expectations about how widows are supposed to be and act.

Nonwidowed readers who buy memoirs by widows or watch emerging movies and TV shows are changing the lens through which they view and judge women who have been through one of the most devastating of losses. These popular culture widows are allowed to lie, cheat, and steal. They make bad decisions as often as they make good ones. They adopt unsavory habits. In other words, they get to have interesting lives that look more authentic and honest. To recognize the audacity of that is to underscore how deep in the shadows our world pushes women after they lose a partner.

Just as there is no right way to be a widow, our interviews with widows make clear that there is also no single path to romance for women who want to reset their lives after the death of a partner. Some widows want marriage, others don't. They want freedom, including from the commitment outlined in traditional marriage vows. They are willing to step away from the expectations of family and friends to design a customized next chapter that incorporates the quirkiness and needs and new people in their next chapter. They need relationships and they are building a rich spectrum of them, not always involving romance.

That is not to say the second time is necessarily easy. Nor is the journey to new love the same for every woman. Widowhood stretches across a broad spectrum. What is universal is that widows have to run a more complex obstacle course than most people seeking romantic love. Not only do they have to put in the work to find a new mate, but they also have to tap their resilience to open their hearts again, to return to what feels normal and recognizable.

The exhilaration of that sprint and the fearlessness of widows taking that chance are testaments to the enduring lure of love in all its shapes and forms. A lot of movies have sequels. Why not yours?

FROM MARTI'S BLOG

One Story from the Life of a Widow

My husband loved our kids, he loved me, and he loved sports and games— maybe in that order. He loved lots of other people and things as well, but with no particular ranking. This is a preface to what my kids and I did recently.

Tom never gave up the fight to beat terminal brain cancer, but his brain and body would not cooperate. So despite his remarkable efforts and positive attitude, the disease rendered him unable to be logical over time. This meant he would not address the fact that he might not make it. We never discussed his funeral wishes. A few times I almost went there, but it was too difficult.

When he died, the kids and I came up with a funeral we thought he might like. As it turned out, it was the kind of funeral I would like. After all, funerals are for the living, right?

I'm Catholic and I raised our children Catholic, so I had a funeral Mass, a eulogy by Tom's best friend (who did a tremendous job), and meaningful read- ings and hymns. Tom was agnostic, but was raised Catholic, so I figured he'd be good with what we planned.

The kids and I felt the funeral had just the right tone and so did family and friends. More than five hundred people attended. Afterward, we had a modest reception with beverages and appetizers in the church basement. At night, we had dinner with immediate family and best friends at a restaurant Tom liked. I knew for sure that he would have loved our gathering, and his presence was felt there.

The funeral was in February. We wanted to do a memorial of some sort and came up with a party at a friend's bar or a chili cook-off (we hosted those regularly). But that first year, I could not move forward with either idea. Another year passed, but it still bothered me I didn't do anything. I had to take action.

Tom loved baseball and coached Little League and Babe Ruth at our city ball fields for fifteen years. A whole group of boys, my son and daughter's ages, grew up on those sports fields a half a block from our house. Some were more talented than others. Tom, in his often loud, always enthusiastic voice, taught them the finer points of baseball and good sportsmanship. He mentored some of the more troubled kids, and even the weakest player was encouraged.

Many of those boys are fine young men today. When Tom was sick, they came over to give him a baseball hat signed by as many of his former players as they could find. It was a touching visit.

Tom never gave up that passion for teaching and watching kids play sports. He coached our daughter in soccer and our son in hockey as well. A solid tennis player, he taught both kids how to play the game well. Our daughter ended up playing high school tennis; our son played three varsity high school sports.

Before he became severely sick, he often walked up to the fields to see what was going on—catch a few innings of the games with kids now younger than his own. When he could no longer walk, I'd drive him around the neighborhood park, which also had the high school tennis courts.

What I needed to do became crystal clear. I called my contact with our city foundation and ordered a bronze plaque. It was installed on the brick column that marks the entrance that Tom and our son entered to go to practice and games. It looks perfect there.

One summer night just before dusk, the kids and I took the urn with Tom's ashes and sprinkled them carefully over the baseball fields. We did it with light hearts and with my son sharing a few fond memories of his many years playing ball and being coached by his father as well as other dads.

The sports fields continue to serve as the cemetery for Tom. Sometimes I sit in one of the dugouts to talk to him or, as I walk by, I lovingly place my hand on one of the two bronze plaques with his name on a field post. It gives me comfort.

Epilogue

There is buoyancy and joy and resilience woven through *Finding Love after Loss*. There is also sadness. Indeed, this book—a multiyear project—is bookended by funerals. The first was that of Tom, the much-loved life partner of Marti, this book's coauthor.

The last was that of Marti herself.

Marti Benedetti, whose widowhood blog inspired this book, died before *Finding Love after Loss* was published. She was diagnosed with cancer immediately after the book project launched, and she carried her disease—managing it, fighting it, cursing it, accommodating it—through the interviews and research for the book, through the writing and editing, through the rewriting and more editing. She proofed the pages before the manuscript went to the publisher and her vote decided the book's cover art. But she did not live to see the book's publication.

Unfortunately, her cancer reawakened just months before the book would appear in bookstores.

Even before her doctors broke the news, Marti suspected the cancer was active again. There were days that she felt less and less well. But she hoped there would be another treatment waiting in the wings. Because that's how her disease operated. The therapies worked for a while, and then they didn't. Each time she exhausted a treatment option, Marti pivoted and a new course of treatment began. For nearly four years that approach worked.

Marti remained her relentless, smart, funny, observant, sardonic, creative self as she plowed ahead on *Finding Love after Loss*. She continued her usual work as a freelance writer even while managing the book project and her health challenges. She was active in her book club.

She stuck to her movie group. She joyfully saw her son, and then her daughter, married to partners she valued, and she welcomed a beautiful granddaughter with piercing blue eyes and, just maybe, a touch of Marti's personality.

Marti also lived through the scary isolation of a pandemic, made even more perilous by her compromised immune system.

During all this, she stayed committed to her belief that the richness in life comes from the relationships we forge and build.

The death of Tom, Marti's husband, crushed her. Widowed while still in her fifties, Marti climbed out of the grief and kept close to old friends while making new friends to match her new life circumstances. She also began to explore what life beyond loss could look like. She dated. She watched her widow and widower friends enter new relationships. She reflected—with wit, sometimes with cynicism or disappointment, and always with a keen eye—on what it is like to welcome love again.

Marti felt strongly that the book she so tenaciously worked on and pushed forward would be useful to women just like her, women whose lives were upended by death. Although she did not survive to see the book published, just days before her death she celebrated that *Finding Love after Loss* was available for presale from online booksellers.

The first presale purchase we knew of was by Marti's daughter-in-law. She bought a copy as a gift for her husband, Marti's son, whose birthday fell on the exact same day the book would be available. Marti applauded that coincidence.

In her final days, too weak to work at the computer, Marti dictated to a friend what would be her final widow's blog post. Since snapshots of her widowhood journey anchor each chapter of *Finding Love after Loss*, it seemed only fitting that her last blog entry should end the book.

FROM MARTI'S BLOG

Finding Love after Loss: A Coda

> *We did it, we completed our book,* Finding Love after Loss.
> *The process has been a long road, just about as long as I have had metastatic breast cancer. The book will be published this fall.*

I'm taking comfort in having completed the book, as I hope it will help others in the future as they try to make their way through the dating landscape.

It's a handbook for dating after widowhood, told from my perspective [as a widow] and the perspective of Mary A. Dempsey, my coauthor who had a longtime relationship with a widower. This blog—LifeAfterWidowhood—was the inspiration for the book.

We still can't believe our good luck in finding a publisher. Many writers pursue publishers and nothing ever happens, but we're the exception to that rule.

My severe health problems have become more grave and that has taken some of the joy from the whole process. I am trying to hold on to the positive aspects of our good fortune.

It has been a challenge to deal with severe cancer without Tom, my dear partner for twenty-eight years, but my children have been my rock in coping with some of this nightmare. As this horrible disease becomes more treacherous, I am aware that my time is running out.

I'm not sure how many entries I will have left in this blog, but it heartens me that my thoughts and work on the subject will live on with Finding Love after Loss: A Relationship Roadmap for Widows.

Notes

CHAPTER 1

1. Amanda King, "Widowed Couple in 80s Set Wedding Date after Online Meeting," *Augusta Chronicle*, December 11, 2020, https://www.augustachron icle.com/story/news/local/2020/12/11/widowed-couple-in-80-s-to-marry -after-meeting-on-dating-site/3880576001.

2. The Legacy Project, https://legacyproject.human.cornell.edu.

3. The National Marriage Project, http://nationalmarriageproject.org/.

CHAPTER 2

1. Gretchen Livingston, "Four-in-Ten Couples Are Saying 'I Do' Again," Pew Research Center, November 14, 2014, https://www.pewsocialtrends.org /wp-content/uploads/sites/3/2014/11/2014-11-14_remarriage-final.pdf.

2. Carole Brody Fleet, "The Epic Struggle: Death vs. Divorce," *HuffPost*, March 24, 2014, https://www.huffpost.com/entry/loss-of-a-spouse_b_4990809.

3. Jiaquan Xu, Sherry L. Murphy, Kenneth D. Kochanek, and Elizabeth Arias. "Mortality in the United States, 2018," NCHS Data Brief No. 355, National Center for Health Statistics, January 2020, https://www.cdc.gov /nchs/data/databriefs/db355-h.pdf.

4. According to the US Census Bureau, the average marriage in the United States lasts eight years. Rose M. Kreider and Renee Ellis, "Number, Timing and Duration of Marriages: 2009," US Census Household Economics Studies, May 2011, https://www.census.gov/prod/2011pubs/p70-125.pdf.

5. Amanda Barusch, *Love Stories of Later Life: A Narrative Approach to Under-standing Later Life* (New York: Oxford University Press, 2008).

6. Loraine A. West, Samantha Cole, Daniel Goodkind, and Wan He, "65+ in the United States: 2010," US Census Bureau, June 2014, https://www.census .gov/content/dam/Census/library/publications/2014/demo/p23-212.pdf.

7. C. Ryan Dunn, "Young Widows' Grief: A Descriptive Study of Personal and Contextual Factors Associated with Conjugal Loss," All Graduate Theses and Dissertations, 2015; 4537, https://digitalcommons.usu.edu/etd/4537.

CHAPTER 3

1. Emmie Griffins, "Judi Dench Opens Up about Love Life: I Don't Like the Word 'Partner,'" *Hello!* August 24, 2020, https://www.hellomagazine.com /celebrities/2020082495908/judi-dench-love-life-relationship-david/.

2. Roxanne Roberts, "Diane Rehm Is Getting Married Again. No One Is More Surprised Than She Is," *Washington Post*, April 27, 2017, https://www .washingtonpost.com/lifestyle/style/diane-rehm-is-getting-married-again-no -ones-more-surprised-than-she-is/2017/04/27/1dd258e6-2b62-11e7-a616 -d7c8a68c1a66_story.html.

3. Vincent M. Mallozzi, "Gertrude Mokotoff, Ex-Mayor and a Bride at 98, Is Dead at 100," *New York Times*, October 23, 2018, https://www.nytimes .com/2018/10/23/obituaries/gertrude-mokotoff-ex-mayor-and-a-bride-at -98-is-dead-at-100.html.

4. Matthew Barbour, "Knitting Widow Finds Love Again after Her Passion for Wool Helped Her Cope with the Death of Her Husband," *Mirror*, September 8, 2018, https://www.mirror.co.uk/news/real-life-stories/knitting-widow -finds-love-again-13212246.

5. Anne Ford, "From the Library with Love," *American Libraries Magazine*, November 1, 2019, https://americanlibrariesmagazine.org/2019/11/01/from -the-library-with-love-online-dating/.

CHAPTER 4

1. Isaac Oliver, "Dating 6 Men at 68: The Woman behind the Musical 'Curvy Widow,'" *New York Times*, September 3, 2017, https://www.nytimes .com/2017/09/03/theater/curvy-widow-bobby-goldman.html.

2. "Tiny Love Stories: I Kept Falling in Love with Other People," *New York Times*, April 2, 2019, https://www.nytimes.com/2019/04/02/style/tiny -modern-love-stories-i-kept-falling-in-love-with-other-people.html.

3. Emily Ladau, "Playing the Online Dating Game, in a Wheelchair," *New York Times*, September 27, 2017, https://www.nytimes.com/2017/09/27/opinion/online-dating-disability.html.

4. M. B. Eberly, E. C. Holley, M. D. Johnson, and T. R. Mitchell, "It's Not Me, It's Not They, It's Us! An Empirical Examination of Relational Attributions," *Journal of Applied Psychology* 102, no. 4 (2017): 711–31, https://psycnet.apa.org/doiLanding?doi=10.1037%2Fapl0000187.

CHAPTER 5

1. "How Many People Broke Quarantine to Have Sex? Our New Survey Has the Answers," Everlywell News and Info, https://www.everlywell.com/blog/news-and-info/survey-sex-during-quarantine/.

2. NYC Health, "Safer Sex and COVID-19," July 8, 2020, https:www1.nyc.gov/assets/doh/downloads/pdf/imm/covid-sex-guidance.pdf.

3. Valerio Capraro and Hélène Barcelo, "The Effect of Messaging and Gender on Intentions to Wear a Face Covering to Slow Down COVID-19 Transmission," PsyArXiv Preprints, May 16, 2020, https://psyarxiv.com/tg7vz/.

4. https://www.facebook.com/groups/377814266290601.

CHAPTER 6

1. Jacob Bernstein, "On Safari in Widowhood," *New York Times*, February 26, 2014, https://www.nytimes.com/2014/02/27/fashion/carole-radziwill-new-novel-the-widows-guide-to-sex-and-dating.html.

2. "Sexuality in Later Life," National Institute on Aging, accessed December 17, 2020, https://www.nia.nih.gov/health/sexuality-later-life.

3. "HIV and Older Americans," Centers for Disease Control and Prevention, accessed December 17, 2020, https://www.cdc.gov/hiv/group/age/older-americans/index.html.

4. https://www.cdc.gov/std/prevention/screeningreccs.htm.

5. "Strategies for Staying Sexual after Menopause," National Women's Health Network, accessed December 17, 2020, https://www.nwhn.org/strategies-for-staying-sexual-after-menopause/.

6. Preeti Malani and Erica Solway, "Let's Talk about Sex," National Poll on Healthy Aging, University of Michigan, May 2018, https://www.healthyagingpoll.org/report/lets-talk-about-sex.

CHAPTER 7

1. American Psychological Association, "Religion or Spirituality Has Positive Impact on Romantic/Marital Relationships, Child Development, Research Shows," News release, 2014, https://www.apa.org/news/press/releases/2014/12/religion-relationships.

2. Michael Langlais and Siera Schwanz, "Religiosity and Relationship Quality of Dating Relationships: Examining Relationship Religiosity as a Mediator," MDPI, September 13, 2017, https://www.mdpi.com/2077-1444/8/9/187.

3. "The Age Gap in Religion around the World," Pew Research Center, June 13, 2018, https://www.pewforum.org/2018/06/13/the-age-gap-in-religion-around-the-world/.

4. American Enterprise Institute, "Partisan Attachment: How Politics Is Changing Dating and Relationships in the Trump Era," February 6, 2020, https://www.aei.org/research-products/report/partisan-attachment-how-politics-is-changing-dating-and-relationships-in-the-trump-era/.

5. "Cranky Coupledom," *Ohio State Insights*, Ohio State University, September 2017, https://insights.osu.edu/life/cranky-couples-tossing-and-turning.

CHAPTER 8

1. Natalie Oliveri, "Sheryl Sandberg Reveals She Was Trolled Online When She Started Dating after Husband's Death," 9Honey program, 9Now, Nine Network, Sydney, Australia, March 2020, https://honey.nine.com.au/latest/sheryl-sandberg-says-she-was-trolled-when-she-started-dating-after-husbands-death/39372d3e-a2a5-4dec-8204-e7d775ccb579.

CHAPTER 9

1. UK Government, "PM Launches Government's First Loneliness Strategy," News release, October 15, 2018, https://www.gov.uk/government/news/pm-launches-governments-first-loneliness-strategy/.

2. "Loneliness Found to Be Strong Predictor of Premature Death," Health Europa.eu, June 11, 2018, https://www.healtheuropa.eu/loneliness-premature-death/86454/.

3. Sara Wilcox, Aaron Aragaki, Charles P. Mouton, Kelly R. Evenson, Sylvia Wassertheil-Smoller, and Barbara Lee Loevinger, "The Effects of Widowhood

on Physical and Mental Health, Health Behaviors, and Health Outcomes: The Women's Health Initiative," *Health Psychology* 22, no. 5 (2003): 513–22, https://www.apa.org/pubs/journals/releases/hea-225513.pdf.

4. Dunn, "Young Widows' Grief."

CHAPTER 10

1. Sun Trust, "First Comes Love, Then Comes . . . Money Squabbles?" accessed December 18, 2020, https://www.suntrust.com/resource-center/personal -finances/article/first-comes-love-then-comes-money-squabbles#.X5q1PC 2ZM1g.

2. Match.com, "Singles in America," accessed December 18, 2020, www .multivu.com/players/English/8264851-match-singles-in-america-study/.

3. Andrea Hasler and Annamaria Lusardi, "The Gender Gap in Financial Literacy: A Global Perspective," Global Financial Literacy Center, July 2017, https://gflec.org/wp-content/uploads/2017/05/The-Gender-Gap-in-Finan cial-Literacy-A-Global-Perspective-Report.pdf?x46739.

4. The National Marriage Project, http://nationalmarriageproject.org.

5. Jeffrey Dew, "The Association between Consumer Debt and the Likelihood of Divorce," *Journal of Family and Economic Issues* 34 (2011): 554–65, https://doi.org/10.1007/s10834-011-9274-z.

CHAPTER 11

1. Renee Stepler, "Number of U.S. Adults Cohabiting with a Partner Continues to Rise, Especially among Those 50 and Older," Pew Research Center, April 6, 2017, https://www.pewresearch.org/fact-tank/2017/04/06/number -of-u-s-adults-cohabiting-with-a-partner-continues-to-rise-especially-among -those-50-and-older/.

2. Claire M. Noël-Miller, "Partner Caregiving in Older Cohabiting Couples," *Journal of Gerontology* 66B, no. 3 (May 2011): 341–53, https://www.ncbi .nlm.nih.gov/pmc/articles/PMC3078761.

3. Sandra Block, "The Financial Pros and Cons of Getting Married Later in Life," *Kiplinger*, December 1, 2015, https://www.kiplinger.com/article/retire ment/t065-c000-s002-pros-and-cons-of-getting-married-later-in-life.html.

4. D'vera Cohn and Jeffrey S. Passel, "A Record 64 Million Americans Live in Multigenerational Households," Pew Research Center, April 5, 2018,

https://www.pewresearch.org/fact-tank/2018/04/05/a-record-64-million -americans-live-in-multigenerational-households/.

5. Jesse Owen, Galena K. Rhoades, and Scott M. Stanley, "Sliding versus Deciding in Relationships: Associations with Relationship Quality, Commitment, and Infidelity," *Journal of Couple and Relationship Therapy* 12, no. 2 (April 1, 2013): 135–49. https://www.ncbi.nlm.nih.gov/pmc/articles/PMC3656416/.

CHAPTER 12

1. Wendy Wang and Kim Parker, "Record Share of Americans Have Never Married," Pew Research Center, September 24, 2014, https://www.pewsocial trends.org/2014/09/24/record-share-of-americans-have-never-married/.

2. Zosia Bielski, "The New Reality of Dating over 65: Men Want to Live Together; Women Don't," *The Globe and Mail*, November 30, 2019, https:// www.theglobeandmail.com/life/relationships/article-women-older-than -65-dont-want-to-live-with-their-partners/.

3. Natalia Sarkisian and Naomi Gerstel, "Does Singlehood Isolate or Integrate? Examining the Link between Marital Status and Ties to Kin, Friends, and Neighbors," *Journal of Social and Personal Relationships* 33, no. 3 (August 3, 2015): 365–84, https://journals.sagepub.com/doi/full/10.1177/0265407515597564.

4. Ashley E. Ermer and Christine M. Proulx, "Associations between Social Connectedness, Emotional Well-Being, and Self-Rated Health among Older Adults: Differences by Relationship Status," *Research on Aging* 4, no. 4 (November 28, 2018): 336–61, https://journals.sagepub.com/doi/abs/10.1177 /0164027518815260.

5. Administration for Community Living, 2018 Profile of Older Americans, April 2018, https://acl.gov/sites/default/files/Aging and Disability in America /2018OlderAmericansProfile.pdf.

6. Cancer.net, "Dating and Intimacy," October 2018, https://www.cancer .net/navigating-cancer-care/dating-sex-and-reproduction/dating-and-intimacy.

Bibliography

Accettura, P. Mark. *Blood and Money: Why Families Fight over Inheritance and What to Do About It*. Farmington Hills, MI: Collinwood Press, 2011.

Ahern, Cecilia. *PS, I Love You*. London: HarperCollins, 2004.

Aikman, Becky. *Saturday Night Widows: The Adventures of Six Friends Remaking Their Lives*. New York: Broadway Books, 2013.

Alpert, Susan Covell. *Driving Solo: Dealing with Grief and the Business of Financial Survival*. N.p.: Barana Books, 2013.

Ansari, Aziz. *Modern Romance: An Investigation*. New York: Penguin Press, 2015.

Armstrong, Alexandra, and Mary R. Donahue. *On Your Own: A Widow's Passage to Emotional and Financial Well-Being*. N.p.: Dearborn, 1993.

Barusch, Amanda. *Love Stories of Later Life: A Narrative Approach to Understanding Later Life*. New York: Oxford University Press, 2008.

Bergen, Candice. *A Fine Romance*. New York: Simon & Schuster, 2014.

Byrne, Anna. *A Widow's Guide: Your Legal and Financial Guide to Surviving the First Year*. Kalamazoo, MI: Flower Press Publishing, 2016.

Catron, Mandy Len. *How to Fall in Love with Anyone: A Memoir in Essays*. New York: Simon & Schuster, 2017.

DePaulo, Bella. *How We Live Now: Redefining Home and Family in the 21st Century*. New York: Atria Books/Beyond Words, 2015.

Didion, Joan. *The Year of Magical Thinking*. New York: Vintage Books, 2007.

Grafman, Keith. *The Art of Instant Message: Be Yourself, Be Confident, Be Successful Communicating Personality*. Highland City, FL: Rainbow Books, 2016.

Juska, Jane. *A Round-Heeled Woman: My Late-Life Adventures in Sex and Romance*. New York: Villard, 2007.

Keogh, Abel. *The Ultimate Dating Guide for Widowers*. N.p.: Ben Lomond Press, 2014.

Klinenberg, Eric. *Going Solo: The Extraordinary Rise and Surprising Appeal of Living Alone*. New York: Penguin Press, 2012.

Krasnow, Iris. *Sex After . . . Women Share How Intimacy Changes as Life Changes.* New York: Gotham Books, 2015.

Lewis, C. S. *A Grief Observed.* London: Faber and Faber, 2015.

Mattlin, Ben. *In Sickness and in Health: Love, Disability, and a Quest to Understand the Perils and Pleasures of Interabled Romance.* Boston: Beacon Press, 2018.

Maynard, Joyce. *The Best of Us: A Memoir.* New York: Bloomsbury, 2017.

McInerny, Nora. *The Hot Young Widows Club.* New York: TEDbooks, 2019.

Mendoza, Marilyn. *We Do Not Die Alone: Jesus Is Coming to Get Me in a White Pickup Truck.* N.p.: ICAN Publishing, 2008.

Oates, Joyce Carol. *A Widow's Story: A Memoir.* N.p.: Ecco Press, 2012.

O'Donohue, John. *Benedictus.* London: Bantam Press, 2007.

Pillemer, Karl. *30 Lessons for Living: Advice from the Wisest Americans on Love, Relationships, and Marriage.* New York: Penguin Group, 2015.

Porter, Max. *Grief Is the Thing with Feathers.* London: Faber & Faber, 2015.

Price, Joan. *Sex after Grief: Navigating Your Sexuality after Losing Your Beloved.* Coral Gables, FL: Mango Publishing Group, 2019.

Quinn, Sally. *Finding Magic: A Spiritual Memoir.* San Francisco: HarperOne, 2017.

Radziwill, Carole. *A Widow's Guide to Sex and Dating.* N.p.: Brillance Audio, 2014.

Rehm, Diane. *On My Own.* New York: Knopf Doubleday Publishing Group, 2016.

Rosenthal, Jason B. *My Wife Said You May Want to Marry Me.* New York: HarperCollins, 2020.

Sandberg, Sheryl, and Adam Grant. *Option B: Facing Adversity, Building Resilience and Finding Joy.* New York: Knopf Doubleday Publishing Group, 2017.

Santlofer, Jonathan. *The Widower's Notebook: A Memoir.* New York: Penguin Random House, 2018.

Traister, Rebecca. *All the Single Ladies: Unmarried Women and the Rise of an Independent Nation.* New York: Simon & Schuster, 2016.

Watson, Anne L. *Living Apart Together.* Friday Harbor, ME: Shepard Publications, 2016.

Weigel, Moira. *Labor of Love: The Invention of Dating.* New York: Farrar, Straus and Giroux, 2016.

White, Richard. *Cybercrime: The Madness behind the Methods.* CreateSpace, 2018.

Index

About the Authors

Marti Benedetti, a widow, lived most of her life in the Detroit area. After an early career as a newspaper reporter, she became a self-employed journalist and corporate writer and researcher. She reported extensively for *Crain's Detroit Business* and other publications. Marti earned a bachelor of arts in journalism from Michigan State University. *Finding Love after Loss* is interspersed with essays from her blog, lifeafter widowhood.wordpress.com. In 2021, after completing the book manuscript but before its publication, Marti died of metastatic breast cancer.

Mary A. Dempsey spent many years working for newspapers and magazines in the United States and Latin America. She now edits and writes for universities, nonprofits, and international think tanks. She has a bachelor's of journalism from the University of Missouri and a master's in political science from the University of Michigan. She lives in a book-filled house across the street from a public library in Washington, DC.